Dark Night Spirituality

Dark Night Spirituality

THOMAS MERTON
DIETRICH BONHOEFFER
ETTY HILLESUM

Contemplation and the New Paradigm

Peter King

First published 1995
SPCK
Holy Trinity Church
Marylebone Road
LONDON
NW1 4DU

British Library Cataloguing in Publication Data
A catalogue record for this book is available from the
British Library.

ISBN 0-281-04884-3

Typeset by Pioneer Associates Perthshire
Printed in Great Britain by
Redwood Books Trowbridge, Wiltshire

Dedicated
to the
memory of my parents
and for
Valerie, Nicholas and Felicity
with love

Contents

vii

Acknowledgements

I would like to thank all who have helped me in the birthing of this work: Bristol Baptist College, where I was prepared for ministry, and Bristol University with whom I wrote my M. Litt. thesis on the spirituality of Merton and Bonhoeffer; the church family of Eynsham Baptist Church where I am at present minister; the many and various individuals with whom I have discussed different aspects of the thoughts and ideas expressed in this book; and especially my wife Valerie and our children Nicholas and Felicity, who have indulged and endured the budding author in their midst!

Some of the material in chapters 1 and 2 was included in a lecture delivered at the Downside Symposium in April 1992 and subsequently published in the *Downside Review*, July 1992, under the title 'A Baptist Looks at Thomas Merton'. Material from chapters 1, 2, 3 and 5 was originally presented in a seminar paper entitled 'Bonhoeffer the Contemplative', given at the International Bonhoeffer Conference in New York City, August 1992.

Finally, I would like to thank my editors at SPCK, Brendan Walsh and Rachel Boulding, for their encouragement and wise counsel.

Peter C. King

1

Impasse or Kairos?

> Right now the whole world seems to be going
> through a dark night of the soul.
> *Flannery O'Connor*

There seem to be two forces at work in our time. On the one hand, things are falling apart – nations, communities and Churches are fragmenting. In both religion and politics, forms of fundamentalism are taking hold. Difference, separateness and individuality are to the fore. Yet at the same time, we are increasingly aware of our common interests as nation states and as a planet. People are yearning to belong; they long for community and connectedness. As the traditional Churches continue in decline, the New Age movement increases in popularity and influence.

For some, the present offers an impasse. The Decade of Evangelism is seen by many as a last-ditch response to this impasse by an increasingly desperate and defensive Church. Yet must impasse necessarily be something negative? Can we not discern in the signs of the times the voice of God – what the New Testament refers to as a *kairos*, a time of opportunity?

As Flannery O'Connor observed many years ago, the whole world seems to be going through a dark night of the soul. For St John of the Cross, the dark night was a profoundly personal and individual experience. It was a stage on one's journey towards God. For us it has become a social and corporate reality, embodied in our society, our culture and our history.

Perhaps the culmination of this process is the intellectual phenomenon called deconstructive postmodernism. In this connection, Charlene Spretnak speaks of the current and pervasive sense that our culture is living through a time of great loss:

> We hear about astonishing rates of species loss . . . Community and family ties have been weakened. The entire stream of human culture . . . has been reduced for most of our young people to the two-dimensional, extremely limited stream of images that appear and disappear on the television screen . . .[1]

Thomas Oden, similarly, speaks of the four characteristics of what he terms decadent modernity: autonomous individualism; narcissistic hedonism; reductive naturalism; and absolute moral relativism.[2]

It is clear that for many people in our time the traditional forms and expressions of faith are no longer meaningful. For the 'death of God' theologian, William Hamilton, 'there is a hole where God used to be', and although 'language about the Christian God is [not] deemed perpetually impossible', its return is not expected or even desired.[3] For St John of the Cross, however, its return would most certainly be expected. The dark night is not to be dismissed as an impasse, but rather embraced as a *kairos* – the way in to a new and more profound experience of God.

St John of the Cross was a product of the catholic mystical tradition. He lived from 1542 to 1591 and was co-founder, with St Teresa of Avila, of a reformed

Carmelite order called the Discalced Carmelites. The central concern of John's writings is the traditional mystical quest for the reality of God. For John, this quest led behind all human words, concepts and imaginings of God, to God Godself. In the *Ascent of Mount Carmel*, John writes that true love for God is 'to labour to divest and deprive oneself for God of all that is not God'.[4] The most enduring image of John's writings is that of the dark night of the soul. This image has found its way into the vocabulary of the Church, and into the awareness of many to whom John himself is virtually unknown. It is undoubtedly true that John analysed and put into words a perennial reality of Christian experience.

At its most basic, the dark night of the soul describes an experience of God which transcends any words, concepts or images of God, and rests in God alone. It is, in a sense, the most radical iconoclasm; even previously cherished images of God are left behind as obstacles on the journey. It is an act of grace and not a human work or achievement, although it is not attained without active willingness on the part of the subject. It is also a mark of spiritual and personal maturity. As John observes: 'God now has taken from this soul its swaddling clothes . . . He has put it down from His arms and is making it walk alone.'[5] In a wider context, the dark night is one expression of what is often referred to as the *via negativa* or negative way. This approach to human discourse about the divine recognises the total inadequacy of any human language to such a task. It is best understood in opposition to the so-called affirmative way, in which God's attributes are regarded as the perfection of human virtues, and God's will is identified with human aspirations. The negative way is characteristic of much of the mystical tradition. The affirmative way is characteristic

3

of much of the liberal tradition. In the words of Thomas Merton:

> The Christian contemplative . . . is called mainly to penetrate the wordless darkness and apophatic light of an experience beyond concepts, and here he gradually becomes familiar with a God who is 'absent' and as it were 'non-existent', to all human experience.[6]

By contrast, Martin Luther King captures the essential thrust of the affirmative way:

> To say that this God is personal is not to make him a finite object besides other objects or attribute to him the limitations of human personality; it is to take what is finest and noblest in our consciousness and affirm its perfect existence in him.[7]

However, such optimism has not always proved well-founded. War, famine, genocide and numerous other crises have dented the optimistic view of a society constantly advancing and improving. And so, because profound questions have been raised about humanity, similar questions have also been raised about the existence, nature and character of God. Maybe God is dead. If not, perhaps God is very different from any of our previous imaginings. An example of this questioning can be seen in Jim Garrison's book, *The Darkness of God: Theology After Hiroshima*. He asks:

> Are we willing to accept that God *brings about* what we experience to be intrinsic evil, that from out of the divine pleroma darkness as well as light issues forth, both equally real, both having equal impact upon human reality?[8]

There are various possible responses to the apparent impasse of our time. One way is to ignore it, and to affirm even more enthusiastically the truths of our religion. This is the way of fundamentalism. Another is to give up our religious beliefs in face of the evidence of human inhumanity. This is the way of atheism. Yet another is to reflect again on the resources of our faith. This is the way of contemplation. In the words of Belden C. Lane:

> . . . in a genuine impasse one's accustomed way of acting and living is brought to a standstill. The left side of the brain, with its usual application of linear, analytical, conventional thinking is ground to a halt. The impasse forces us to start all over again, driving us to contemplation. On the other hand, the impasse provides a challenge and a concrete focus for contemplation . . . It forces the right side of the brain into gear, seeking intuitive, symbolic, unconventional answers, so that action can be renewed eventually with greater purpose.[9]

Common Ground

This work arose from the observation that there is some important - though largely unexplored - common ground between the life and thought of American Trappist Thomas Merton, German pastor and theologian Dietrich Bonhoeffer, and Dutch Jewish academic Etty Hillesum - and that this common ground has something to do with their response to the impasse of our century.

Dietrich Bonhoeffer, of course, did not know Thomas Merton. The year the young Merton entered

Gethsemani, the mind of the Lutheran pastor was pre-occupied with other matters, and the monk's first writings had yet to appear. However, Thomas Merton did know of Dietrich Bonhoeffer, and references – most notably to the later Bonhoeffer – are to be found among his writings. Merton himself noted the similarity between Bonhoeffer's later thought and the reflections of St John of the Cross on the dark night of the soul:

> Reading Bonhoeffer's statements in his prison letters in the context of the whole work . . . we can surmise that his 'godless' kenoticism was quite probably the result of a deep personal evolution of his genius and his faith.

Indeed, he notes: 'One might compare it with St John of the Cross.'[10]

Merton very clearly understood himself as standing in the tradition of John. He used John's language and concepts – among others – to describe his journey of faith as a contemplative and a monk. Bonhoeffer, however, coming from a different Christian tradition, did not understand his experience in such terms. Yet the parallels are there: Bonhoeffer's work on *Ethics*, and especially his prison writings, appear to present evidence of an intriguingly similar phenomenon.

Central to this study is the assertion that Dietrich Bonhoeffer underwent a process of Johannine 'purgation' in his final years. This process resulted in a universalizing of faith and a renewed vision of God's presence and reality in the world, to the extent that God came to be seen as less distinct from, and more implicit in, the world. For example, Bonhoeffer could speak of living 'as though God were not given', but also of 'unconscious Christianity'.[11]

Merton did not develop his observation regarding Bonhoeffer and John of the Cross. There was no reason why he should do. For us, however, looking back on both Merton and Bonhoeffer with the perspective of a quarter of a century, there is every reason to do so. We live in an age when there is much interest in the unity of experience behind the diversity of expression both within Christianity itself and between the different world religions.

It seems that there is a very real convergence of thought and action in our tumultuous time, cutting across formerly sacrosanct boundaries of tradition and pointing to the universality of spiritual experience. In this connection, Madonna Kolbenschlag states in an interview in *Sojourners* magazine:

> I think that all of us today are experiencing a distance from our own traditions or denominations because we are becoming aware that the human and material superstructure created around it isn't the essence of the tradition.[12]

In a similar vein, Rosemary Ruether observes in an article discussing various models of Church, and in particular that which she refers to as Liberation Christianity, that: 'Each of these types of Christian may be more comfortable with their counterparts in other denominations than with critics within their own church.'[13]

David Abalos notes a similar phenomenon not just within Christianity but between different religious traditions. Abalos suggests three possible understandings of God's activity in the world:

- God endorses the world as it is ordered at present – the God of emanation.

7

- God enables us to live with the world as it is – the God of incoherence.
- God creates alternatives which offer new and better possibilities – the God of transformation.

Each of these three human concepts of the divine connects us 'in qualitatively different ways to the Source of Sources . . .' The effect of this, continues Abalos, is that 'a Catholic who journeys with the god of transformation has more in common with Hindus, Baptists, or Anglicans who travel with the same god than with a Catholic who is committed to the god of emanation.'[14]

In their respective analyses, both Ruether and Abalos discern what is, in effect, a cross-denominational and cross-religious ecumenism.

Indeed, within Christianity alone, both the charismatic movement and the renewed interest in more traditional spirituality demonstrate an increasing awareness that experience of God cuts across denominational and theological boundaries. This has always been so, yet it is only in recent years that it seems to have been fully appreciated by the Christian community. One significant example of this cross-denominational ecumenism may be found in the common ground shared by two of the subjects of our study: Dietrich Bonhoeffer and Thomas Merton.

The inclusion of a third subject, the Dutch Jewess, Etty Hillesum, indicates the importance of also exploring examples of cross-religious ecumenism. For Etty Hillesum's diaries, written in Nazi-occupied Amsterdam, reveal a strikingly similar perspective to that of the German pastor.

Contemplation

It is easy for any exploration of common ground between religious traditions to end up dealing with very vague and nebulous concepts with very little precision and rational coherence. For this reason, it is suggested here that one specific concept, that of contemplation, forms the common ground between Merton, Bonhoeffer and Hillesum.

Thomas Merton acts as our 'control'. For he, self-avowedly, in his life and work represents the Christian contemplative tradition. Dietrich Bonhoeffer, standing in the Lutheran, Protestant tradition, would have been unlikely to have seen himself as following in the way of Eckhart, John and Teresa – and yet his prison writings demonstrate a clear affinity with their spirituality of contemplation. Etty Hillesum would appear to be an even more unlikely contemplative, and yet her diaries reveal a powerful and profound spirituality that can appropriately be termed contemplative.

Contemplation is about reality – the reality of oneself, of the world, of God. It is about seeing things as they really are, rather than as we have made them or wished them to be. At the root of contemplation, therefore, is an awareness that God and the world are inseparable.

Contemplation is a perspective on the world which does full justice to the uniqueness of each person, the presence of God in all things, and the unity yet diversity of all creation. It leads to persons exploring and becoming the unique human beings they were created to be, and through that uniqueness embodying and expressing God. Contemplation leads to persons exploring the world around them and seeing behind the illusions of autonomy and independence a vision of the fundamental unity of all things in their creator God. It leads to persons exploring their concepts and pictures of God, and letting them go as they glimpse the reality of a God beyond all human attempts at description and representation.

Yet contemplation is no passive exercise. Piercing through to the reality of God leads to action. It leads to action in regard to oneself, to the world, and to one's faith in God. Contemplation leads to change and transformation in oneself, in religious communities, and in the world at large. It leads to a commitment to work to bring things closer to the vision of reality which one has glimpsed.

This is contemplation – and yet it is not. In the end, contemplation defies formulation and description. It remains elusive and open, awaiting a specific human life in a particular context to give it content. And so, three human lives are offered here as examples of what contemplation meant to three very different people in three very different situations. They share definite common ground, but there is also much that is special to each individual. We are interested in both the common ground and the differences.

2

Thomas Merton
'The Unmasking of an Illusion'

Thomas Merton was born in France in 1915. His parents were both artists, his father a New Zealander and his mother an American. In 1916 the family moved to the United States and settled on Long Island near his mother's family. Two years later another son, John Paul, was born, although Tom was to see relatively little of his younger brother. Then, in 1921, Ruth Merton died. Young Tom was not allowed to see his mother during her long hospitalization, and her farewell to him took the form of a letter brought home one day by his father.

Following his mother's death, Tom spent time variously in Bermuda and France with his father, in New York with his brother and grandparents, and in England at boarding school. These years were to leave a lasting mark on him, for during the formative years of childhood and adolescence Tom was never to have the opportunity to form lasting relationships with people or places. After a somewhat dissolute year at Cambridge, during which he fathered an illegitimate child, he returned to the United States and commenced studies at New York's Columbia University.

Thomas Merton was baptized a Roman Catholic in November 1938. Three years later, in December 1941, after a considerable internal struggle over his future vocation, he entered the Trappist Abbey of Gethsemani in Kentucky.

The quarter century which Merton spent in Gethsemani saw vast changes in both Church and society. In the Church, the Second Vatican Council let in the fresh air of change and renewal, and started a ferment which continues to this day. On the wider stage, the world saw the atomic bomb in action and lived from then on in its shadow. In America the civil rights movement received fresh impetus from the leadership of Martin Luther King Jr, and in America, too, the war in Vietnam hastened the coming together of a counterculture.

The life of Thomas Merton is a vivid illustration of the effects of these changes on one man. He entered the monastery a fairly 'typical' monk – typical at least according to our stereotypes – yet by his death he was anything but typical. It took some time for the 'real' Thomas Merton to emerge again out of the unquestioning enthusiasm which characterized his first years in the abbey. Indeed, the process of finding his true identity was to preoccupy Merton in some form or other for the rest of his life. Gradually his eyes were opened to his own humanity, and by the late 1950s he had rediscovered the fact that as a monk he was also a member of the human race.

This manifested itself in a number of ways: in an increasing concern for, and commitment to, issues of peace and justice; in an innocent and profoundly healing love affair with a young nurse; and finally in a growing interest in the spirituality of the East. This culminated in the trip to India and the Far East from which Merton was not to return.

Thomas Merton died in December 1968, as a result of accidental electrocution while attending a monastic conference in Bangkok.

Encountering Reality

It was while he was a student at New York's Columbia University that Merton began to show an interest in Roman Catholicism. A key factor in this awakening of interest was his discovery of Etienne Gilson's book, *The Spirit of Medieval Philosophy*. Gilson's work was something of a surprise, as Walter Conn notes: 'It was a great relief for Merton to discover that no idea or sensible image could contain God, and further that we must not be satisfied with such knowledge of God.'[1]

Some eighteen months later Thomas Merton was baptized a Roman Catholic. Yet that was not going to be the end of it, for in his search for reality he felt increasingly drawn to a religious order. In the end, he was presented with what amounted to a choice between joining Baroness de Hueck Doherty's 'Friendship House' in Harlem, or the Trappist community at the Abbey of Gethsemani near Louisville, Kentucky.

Of 'Friendship House' Merton wrote in a letter: 'What actually inspired me was the idea of complete poverty, *real* poverty, without security . . .'[2] Yet, of Gethsemani he wrote: 'I should tear out all the other pages of this book and all the other pages of everything else I ever wrote, and begin here. This is the center of America. I have wondered what was holding this country together . . . It is this monastery – if only this one.'[3]

And so, on 10 December 1941, Merton entered Gethsemani.

Contemplation

As a member of the Gethsemani community, Merton entered into the tradition and practice of contemplation. His life became a journey of exploration into what it meant to be a contemplative in the modern world. This, too, is a concern of much of his work.

The task of defining contemplation is not easy. In his book, *New Seeds of Contemplation*, Merton writes: 'Contemplation cannot be taught. It can only be hinted at, suggested, pointed to, symbolised.'[4]

Contemplation is a gift of God. As such, it is God's grace and not human effort which produces a contemplative. Yet grace calls forth faith. God reveals Godself, and in faith we say 'yes' to God, resting not in propositions about God, but in God alone. 'If nothing that can be seen can either be God or represent Him to us as He is, then to find God we must pass beyond everything that can be seen and enter into darkness.'[5]

In faith we say 'yes' to God, and after this words, images and concepts fall away until faith rests not on human imaginings about God, but on God. As Merton writes: 'True faith must be able to go on even when everything else is taken away from us.'[6]

Words and images lose their meaning, the superstructure of faith falls away, and yet God is making Godself known in the darkness and desert of God's apparent absence. We come to realize that: 'You are going somewhere and that your journey is guided and directed and that you can feel safe.'[7]

The next stage in the journey is the discovery that we are not alone, but rather that there is an essential unity within all creation. Because of this, Merton is convinced that nothing external to ourselves is in itself an obstacle

14

to our union with God: 'You have to take God and
creatures all together and see God in His creation and
creation in God and don't ever separate them. Then
everything manifests God instead of hiding God or
being in the way of God as an obstacle.'[8]

Solidarity and Illusion

In 1951, Merton took on the post of Master of
Scholastics in the monastery. His new responsibilities
began to break down the self-imposed barriers between
the monk and the world. This process culminated in the
so-called 'Vision in Louisville'. Some time after the
event, Merton wrote of it in a published journal: 'In
Louisville, at the corner of Fourth and Walnut . . . I was
suddenly overwhelmed with the realization that I loved
all those people, that they were mine and I theirs, that
we could not be alien to one another even though we
were total strangers . . .'[9]

Merton was discovering that contemplation is about
unity. The contemplative finds that there is a unity
between him or herself, God, and other people. The
journey towards God inevitably means a journey towards
other people.

Merton worked out the implications of this discovery
in an increasing commitment to the movement for peace
and social justice. He admitted that his community
included those who were active for peace and justice 'out
in the world' as much as it did his fellow monks. As he
wrote to Rosemary Ruether: 'I try as best I can to keep
up valid and living contacts with my friends who are in
the thick of things, and everyone knows where my real
"community" is . . .'[10]

Merton's growing sense of responsibility towards the world outside Gethsemani marked no essential departure from the monastic tradition. However, his outworking of it was something radically new. His vision of the role of the Church *vis-à-vis* society is best captured in his own description of the meaning of the medieval idea of *contemptus mundi*, as 'not the rejection of a reality, but the unmasking of an illusion'.[11]

The contemplative is concerned with clarifying, protesting, demystifying – but not directly with transforming. The goal of the contemplative is the unmasking of the illusion which prevents the fulfilment both of the person and of the world, in Christ. Illusion is sin: it prevents both individual persons and the world from becoming that which they were created to be.

The point from which the process of what we might call 'dis-illusionment' emanates is the Church. The unity which is God's intention for all creation begins to be a reality here and now in the Church. As Merton writes in one of the essays collected in *The Monastic Journey*:

> To have a truly spiritual life is . . . to think and love and act not just as Christ *would* act in a given situation, but as He precisely *does* act, by His grace, in us, at the moment. It is to live and act with the mind of the Church, which is the mind of Christ.[12]

The quest for God, the inward world of personal identity, and the outward world of social and political issues, converge in a common quest for dis-illusionment. The task of the contemplative is to strip away the illusions obscuring a true vision of reality.

Final Integration

The years of Merton's most intense commitment to the issues of war, racism and the nuclear question also marked an episode in his personal life which called into question the validity of his monastic vocation. He fell in love with a young nurse, and yet saw in that love no essential contradiction of his calling. However, Merton's discovery that he too could love and be loved by another human being confronted the whole institutional framework of the monastic vocation with a challenge it could only reject. The monk, it would appear, cannot love in the way Merton loved Margie Smith.

Merton first met Margie Smith during a period of hospitalization for stomach troubles in March 1966. Margie was the nurse who had been allocated to him, and they soon began to find pretexts to be together. What emerged was a mutual need for friendship at a deep, spiritual level. Merton biographer John Howard Griffin believes that they were in love, although they did not at first realize it themselves. On his discharge from hospital, Merton left a letter for Margie with his address, in the obvious hope that the friendship would continue, which it did.

Although the relationship did not appear to have any long-term future, it continued for over two years, with secret – and not so secret – letters, meetings and telephone calls. In Margie, Merton had finally found someone with whom he could share his deepest thoughts and feelings.[13] However, the relationship did indeed have no future, and a last telephone call during the summer of 1968 ended with Merton's hanging up on a note of desperation.[14] There was no way forward.

Despite the fact that Merton's love for Margie Smith was to end in frustration, this episode was a resounding reaffirmation of his humanity as a monk. It was remarkable enough as an experience which is usually denied to monks, and even more so for its coming at a time when Merton was in the throes of making his permanent commitment to the life of a hermit.

The term 'Final Integration' is used by Merton in one of his essays collected in the posthumously published volume, *Contemplation in a World of Action*.[15] Merton's interest in the concept arises from the very real tension, apparent during his last years, between his quest for true identity and his monastic vocation. As a contemplative he believed passionately in finding and realizing his true identity. Yet as one who by his monastic vows was sworn to obedience, he had placed limits on his freedom and decided in advance on certain questions relating to his identity. Thus, for example, marriage was precluded while he remained a monk.

In Merton's own life this tension came to a head both in his writing and in his love for Margie Smith. It is captured in words in a passage where he writes of how the monastic vows 'should deliver the Monk from fixation upon the partial, the limited, the provisional . . .' and then continues: 'But at the same time I am convinced that a monastic life without vows is quite possible and perhaps very desirable.'[16]

In the end, the aim of the monastic community should be the development of the fully integrated person. In his essay Merton draws on the work of Iranian psychotherapist Reza Arasteh, and applies his concept of 'final integration' to the monastic vocation. Of Arasteh's profile of the fully integrated person, he writes: 'He is in a certain sense identified with everybody . . . He is fully

18

"Catholic" in the best sense of the word . . . He has attained to a deep inner freedom . . . He is guided not just by will and reason, but by "spontaneous behavior subject to dynamic insight".'

This is also the aim of the monastic vocation. Merton observes that 'this kind of maturity is exactly what the monastic life should produce'.[17]

The process is one which would also have been familiar to St Benedict, St Bernard and St John of the Cross. For the movement towards 'final integration' follows a pattern 'of disintegration, existential moratorium and reintegration on a higher, universal level [which] is precisely what the monastic life is meant to provide'.[18]

However, it is all too obvious to Merton that the implications of such a personal and communal process would not find favour in the monastery. Indeed, the effect might be 'revolutionary'. 'Hence . . . our community life is unconsciously organised to make sure that any such development will be subject to human control.'[19]

Sadly, Merton's life and work were cut short by his untimely death. Precisely where his growing concern for 'final integration' would have led him we cannot know. During the course of his last address in Bangkok on the day of his death, he told a story containing what was in his judgement an important monastic statement: 'From now on, Brother, everybody stands on his own two feet.'[20]

It remained Merton's dream that one day a monasticism with radically different structures would be possible. Yet it was not to be during his lifetime. Nevertheless, Thomas Merton's vision for the world, the Church and the monastic vocation continues to point to what might be.

A New Way of Seeing

Some observers were no doubt dismayed when Thomas Merton began to include the events of world history within the scope of his writings. Why should a monk who had entered the monastery in order to leave behind the triviality and illusion of the world suddenly begin to demonstrate solidarity with that same world? How could such a man offer an opinion on the complex issues of our time, let alone commit himself to a political stance? What reason could he possibly have for entering – if only in print – the complex and morally ambiguous arena of social and political affairs?

The answer lies in the life of the man himself. For Merton, it was the monastic vocation itself which led him to commitment to the affairs of the world. He came to believe that he could not continue to be a monk and a contemplative without including the wider world in his life's agenda. His monastic theology of standing apart from the world for the sake of the world would not let him keep silent. There were insights to be shared which were the fruit of his monastic separation. Refusing to recognize or share them would mean becoming the victim of yet another illusion – that the monk was a different kind of human being, or even no human at all!

It was also as a monk and a contemplative that Merton embarked on his quest to the East. Here again, a life rooted in the experience of dis-illusionment had led him to realize that religious exclusivism was as impossible as social and political separatism. The contemplative vision encompassed all reality – not just the spiritual or the Christian.

Thomas Merton's life was a journey of discovery in which, one by one, the illusions of political neutrality and religious sectarianism were stripped away to reveal that there in the world, in its struggles for justice and peace, in its myriad forms of religious expression, is God.

As Merton wrote in a letter to the Indian poet and philosopher, Amiya Chakravarty:

> It is not easy to try to say what I know I cannot say. I do really have the feeling that you have all understood and shared quite perfectly. That you have seen something that I see to be most precious. The reality that is present to us and in us: call it Being, call it Atman, call it Pneuma . . . or Silence. And the simple fact that by being attentive, by learning to listen (or recovering the natural capacity to listen which cannot be learned any more than breathing), we can find ourself engulfed in such happiness that it cannot be explained: the happiness of being at one with everything in that hidden ground of Love for which there can be no explanations.[21]

3

Dietrich Bonhoeffer
'As If God Were Not Given'

Dietrich Bonhoeffer was born in Germany in 1906. His father was a psychiatrist, and his mother's father and grandfather were both theologians. It was a closely-knit, upper middle class family, and that ethos stayed with Bonhoeffer throughout his life. The death of his brother Walter in the First World War made a considerable impact on twelve year-old Dietrich, so much so that his childhood faith in God led him to long for a way to reassure his family that death need not be feared.

In due course Bonhoeffer entered theological studies. Although he was not as yet motivated by any real commitment to the Church or a specific system of beliefs, he was ordained in 1931 as a minister in the Lutheran Church. During the early 1930s, Bonhoeffer underwent the change which his biographer Bethge describes as moving from 'theologian' to 'Christian'. His life and work were marked by a new conviction of the certainties of the Christian faith.[1]

The change was significant. Bonhoeffer's friends and colleagues noticed that for the first time he attended Church services regularly, and that he read the Bible and took its message with great seriousness. Bonhoeffer himself claimed later that the change was brought about because he had become a Christian. Whatever we think of that assertion, it is clear that he had come to a new awareness of faith and that his life had taken on a renewed sense of purpose.

In the 1930s, Bonhoeffer led a community established for the training of ministers in a place called Finkenwalde. His students recall their mentor's concern for spiritual development and his love of life. They would often be sent out into the surrounding countryside to pray and to meditate. At other times they would study or make music together. To prepare for ministry was not to say 'no' to life! Meanwhile, the Nazi regime was tightening its grip on Germany. The time came when the seminary had to continue covertly, and eventually it was closed by the Nazis.

In 1935 the so-called Aryan Clause became law. This prevented Jews from attaining positions of responsibility in the community. Its effect on the Church was to disqualify Jewish Christians from its ministry. Most of those in the established Church went along with this requirement, and indeed with the entire philosophy of Nazism, seeing in it nothing contrary to the way of Christ.

There were, however, some Christians in the established Church who did not fall in with the regime. Known as the 'Confessing Church', they accused the 'German Christians' of capitulating the faith of the Church to a secular philosophy. Because they believed that the integrity of the Church's message was at stake, the Confessing Church separated itself off from the main body of compromisers.

Despite this apparently radical action, Bonhoeffer remained profoundly dissatisfied. The Confessing Church, it seemed, was concerned only with itself. As long as the Church was able to be the Church – pure and pristine –

in charge of its own affairs, drawing its own boundaries, defining its own beliefs, it was satisfied. What Bonhoeffer wanted to see, however, was the Confessing Church standing up for others!

Face to face with the realities of the Nazi regime, Bonhoeffer underwent another change – from what Bethge describes as 'Christian' to 'contemporary'. He could no longer ignore the very real and complex demands of Christian life and witness in Hitler's Germany. His commitment to discipleship had led him to the point where things were going to be very different – both in faith and in life. In 1939 Bonhoeffer joined the Abwehr, the German Military Intelligence. This was an organization which was not as yet run by the Nazis. Under the cover of various assignments, agent Bonhoeffer travelled throughout Europe, among the Churches, representing both the German resistance against Hitler and the ecumenical movement.

During this time, Bonhoeffer made a number of unsuccessful approaches to the allies on behalf of a group of anti-Nazi conspirators who planned to kill Hitler and take over the country. Those who made up the group held influential positions in the military and in society in general, and were aware that they should have done much more to prevent the rise of Hitler and the Nazi regime. They plotted to assassinate Hitler, after which a coup would unseat the Nazis and force a negotiated surrender.

Dietrich Bonhoeffer was arrested in April 1943 and taken to Tegel Military Prison in Berlin. Various charges were mentioned during his early months in prison. His exemption from military service came under scrutiny, as did his journeys abroad, together with 'Operation Seven', which had succeeded in helping fourteen Jews to escape the country. In the end, a charge of high treason was dropped and replaced by one of 'sabotage against the armed forces'.

In prison, Dietrich Bonhoeffer continued the writing which had so engaged him before his arrest. From *Ethics* he moved on to fiction and a play, culminating in the intriguing writings later to be collected in *Letters and Papers from Prison*.

On 20 July 1944 a failed attempt was made on Hitler's life. This was the plan which all the conspirators had been working for, and now their conspiracy was blown wide open. Bonhoeffer's hopes that the case against him would eventually run out of steam were soon to be dashed.

That October he was transferred to a Gestapo prison, where he was no longer accorded the privileges of one whose uncle was Lieutenant General of Berlin. In February 1945, he was transferred again, this time to the concentration camp of Buchenwald. On Low Sunday, 8 April 1945, after leading a worship service for his fellow prisoners, Bonhoeffer was finally taken to the concentration camp at Flossenberg. There, following the orders of an enraged Hitler, he was tried and sentenced to death. On the morning of 9 April – barely a month before Hitler's own death – Dietrich Bonhoeffer was executed.

Bonhoeffer's final years were marked by his involvement in conspiracy and subterfuge far removed from what might be expected in the life of a minister of the Church. Yet it was in the midst of the reality of Nazi evil, and the equally real necessity to put an end to that evil, that the young pastor met the call of Christ. For him, the question was not so much whether it was right to become involved in such political activities, but whether it was permissible not to. The burden of proof lay on those who, in the name of Christ and the Church, stayed aloof from opposition to the Nazis.

It is out of this arena of moral and spiritual uncertainty, and in dialogue with all too real and personal situations, that Bonhoeffer's final works were produced. We can only guess at the direction his life and work would have taken had he lived, yet his legacy lives on and continues to challenge us all.

Following Jesus

The 1930s, marked as they were by the rise of Nazism, were a time when the Church was called to utter a clear and unambiguous message – the call to follow Jesus Christ.

Even at this stage in his thought, Bonhoeffer was concerned to avoid presenting a picture of Christianity which implied that it had all the answers to every human situation. In his book *The Cost of Discipleship* he is at pains to stress that following Jesus does not provide a programme for living and acting, nor a standard of right and wrong to apply to others. Rather: 'To follow in [Jesus'] footsteps is something which is void of all content. It gives us no intelligible programme for a way of life, no goal or ideal to strive after. It is not a cause which human calculation might deem worthy of our devotion . . .'[2]

Following Jesus is not in the end about a human decision. As Bonhoeffer writes: 'We cannot transform ourselves into [Christ's] image; it is rather the form of Christ which seeks to be formed in us . . . and to be manifested in us.'[3]

From the outset, Bonhoeffer is concerned to locate

personal discipleship within the community of faith.
The follower of Jesus does so in the context of 'Christ
existing as community'. For the Church is 'Christ
Himself who has taken form among men . . . a section
of humanity in which Christ has really taken form'.
Indeed, the 'true form' of all humanity is that of Jesus
Christ, a form 'which is its own by right, which it has
already received, but which it merely fails to understand
and accept'.[4]

Despite this stress on community, Bonhoeffer says
that the community exists in order that the individuals
who make it up might become mature and free. In his
book *Life Together*, he presents what he calls 'the test of
meditation': 'Has the fellowship served to make the
individual free, strong, and mature, or has it made him
weak and dependent?'[5]

Similarly, with regard to authority within the community, he notes what he sees as a 'hankering for false
authority' through dependence upon fellow human
beings rather than God.[6]

Responsible Action

Central to Bonhoeffer's thought is the claim that God
and the world are united in Christ. Therefore he can
assert that: 'There are not two realities, but only one
reality, and that is the reality of God, which has become
manifest in Christ in the reality of the world.' And of
the Christian that: 'His worldliness does not divide him
from Christ, and his Christianity does not divide him
from the world. Belonging wholly to Christ, he stands at
the same time wholly in the world . . .'[7]

Faced with the complexity of involvement in the
conspiracy against Hitler while working as an agent for

the Abwehr, Bonhoeffer became even more deeply and personally aware that following Jesus did not bring with it a programme of action, determined in advance, which avoided personal responsibility. In his *Ethics* he observes that the responsible person 'is dependent on the man who is concretely his neighbour in his concrete possibility'.

Bonhoeffer does not present an ethics of principle established in advance and applied to each situation, for there is no principle 'which possesses absolute validity . . . [Indeed] the "absolute good" may sometimes be the very worst.'[8]

Therefore, responsible action is grounded in the reality of the current situation, responding to Christ as he is met in the neighbour, yet ultimately ignorant as to its own goodness. Sometimes this will mean that the right course of action in a given situation will be self-evident; at other times it will be anything but evident. And so, in the final analysis, the responsible person 'commits his action into the hands of God and lives by God's grace and favour'.[9]

Impasse and Reconstruction

In his struggle against Nazism, Bonhoeffer experienced the collapse not only of the social and political framework of his life, but also that of his personal life and relationships. For example, he became increasingly isolated from the Confessing Church and his fellow clergy. During these years he came to see life from a very different perspective. 'We have for once', he wrote, 'learnt to see the great events of world history from below . . .'

In what sounds a profoundly modern insight, suffering became the key to understanding the world. And with a new perspective came new claims on him: 'The ultimate question for a responsible man to ask is not how he is to extricate himself heroically from the affair, but how the coming generation is to live.'[10]

Action, not passivity, was needed in response to the impasse in which the German people found themselves under the Nazi regime. Action alone would open up the possibility of a time when the superstructure of faith and morality would again exist in Germany. Robin Lovin describes Bonhoeffer's involvement in the conspiracy as 'a commitment to restructure the situation . . .' because it is imperative that 'Christ must begin to take form again in the structures of human life'.[11]

'As Though God Were Not Given'

Although he did not realize it at the time, Bonhoeffer's imprisonment in Tegel marked the final phase in his life and work. It was in Tegel that he embarked upon what was a completely new venture for him - work on a play and, later, a novel. Perhaps this is evidence of the right brain at work, turning from the analytical and conventional and exploring the intuitive and unconventional. These years also leave us some of Bonhoeffer's most challenging and intriguing theological exploration.

The main themes of Bonhoeffer's prison writings sound a familiar note to the student of St John's dark night: humanity's coming of age; life without God - yet before God; finding God where God chooses to reveal himself; the falling away of all the props to faith; a revisioning of both faith and Church. We shall consider each in turn.

Bonhoeffer refers a number of times in his *Letters and Papers from Prison* to 'the world that has come of age'.[12]

This is his term for a world from which 'God is being increasingly pushed out'.[13] Elsewhere he notes the increasing autonomy of a world for which 'God as a working hypothesis in morals, politics, or science, has been surmounted and abolished'.[14]

It is in just this world that the Christian is called to live *etsi deus non daretur* ('as if God were not given'). As Bonhoeffer writes:

> . . . our coming of age leads us to a true recognition of our situation before God. God would have us know that we must live as men who manage their lives without him . . . Before God and with God we live without God. God lets himself be pushed out of the world on to the cross.[15]

The Christian is to 'find and love God in what he actually gives us'.[16] Thus Bonhoeffer can note in his 'Outline for a Book': 'The transcendent is not infinite and unattainable tasks, but the neighbour who is within reach in any given situation.'[17]

It is to the neighbour that God in Jesus – Bonhoeffer calls him the 'man for others' – points us as we seek a true experience of the transcendent God.

As these far-reaching ideas were germinating in his mind, Bonhoeffer also experienced a personal falling away of the superstructure of faith. In a letter of December 1943, after nearly six months of imprisonment, he wrote: 'By the way, it's remarkable how little I miss going to church. I wonder why?'[18]

Later, in March 1944, he noted: 'Once again I'm having weeks when I don't read the Bible much; I never know quite what to do about it. I have no feeling of obligation about it, and I know, too, that after some time I shall plunge into it again voraciously.'[19]

While it would be unwise to read too much significance into these two brief references, read in the light of the overall direction of Bonhoeffer's thought during his time in prison, they offer a personal context for his increasingly radical thought.

At the end of the process lay the revisioning of faith and Church to which Bonhoeffer pointed in the notes for his never-to-be-written book. A fitting introduction to these notes is his 'Thoughts on the day of the baptism of Dietrich Wilhelm Rüdiger Bethge', written in May 1944. At the end of this long-distance sermon for his nephew's baptism, Bonhoeffer offered the following glimpse into the future as he saw it:

Today you will be baptised a Christian. All those great ancient words of the Christian proclamation will be spoken over you, and the command of Jesus Christ to baptise will be carried out on you, without your knowing anything about it. But we are once again being driven right back to the beginnings of our understanding. Reconciliation and redemption, regeneration and the Holy Spirit, love of our enemies, cross and resurrection, life in Christ and Christian discipleship – all these things are so difficult and so remote that we hardly venture any more to speak of them. In the traditional words and acts we suspect that there may be something quite new and revolutionary, though we cannot as yet grasp or express it . . . Our earlier words are therefore bound to lose their force and cease, and our being Christians today will be limited to two things: prayer and action by the just person on behalf of people. All Christian thinking, speaking, and organising must be born anew out of this prayer and action . . . It is not for us to prophesy the day (though the day will come) when men will once more be called so to utter the word of God that the world will be changed and renewed by it. It will be a new language, perhaps quite nonreligious, but liberating and redeeming – as was Jesus' language; it will shock people and yet overcome them by its power; it will be the language of a new righteousness and truth, proclaiming God's peace with people and the coming of his kingdom . . . Till then the Christian cause will be a silent and hidden affair, but there will be those who pray and do right and wait for God's own time.[20]

Bonhoeffer intended to begin his book with a chapter devoted to what he called 'A Stocktaking of Christianity'. Here the fragmentary references to humanity's 'coming of age' were to have been developed, together with Bonhoeffer's judgement that the German Church of his time was essentially a 'church on the defensive'.[21]

The second chapter was intended to present what he saw as 'The Real Meaning of Christian Faith', starting with the most basic question: 'Who is God?' Again, Bonhoeffer clearly intended to develop ideas he had already floated in his letters. He writes: 'Our relation to God is a new life in "existence for others", through participation in the being of Jesus.'[22]

This chapter would have continued with an interpretation of Christian faith 'on this basis', and would have concluded by posing the vital question: 'What do we really believe? I mean, believe in such a way that we stake our lives on it?'

The third chapter is headed simply 'Conclusions', and it is here that we get a glimpse of the revisioning of the Church which Bonhoeffer saw as following from his reinterpretation of faith: 'The church is the church only when it exists for others'.[24] And so, Bonhoeffer suggests, it should give away all its property to those in need and its clergy should live solely on the financial support of their congregations.

Dietrich Bonhoeffer was never to write that book, and so his vision continues to tantalize us with its very incompleteness. Following Jesus had led to this vision for the future, yet it led also to death at the hands of the Nazis.

Faith or Atheism?

Did Dietrich Bonhoeffer lose his faith in Tegel? Before his imprisonment there had already been raised eyebrows among the pastors of the Confessing Church that the author of *The Cost of Discipleship* should have thrown in his lot with the Abwehr. However, read in the light of the contemplative tradition, Bonhoeffer's later life and writings can be seen as an expression of Johannine purgation. Claims of certainty, separation and innocence are denied as Bonhoeffer becomes more and more aware of both his own solidarity – and God's solidarity in Jesus Christ – with the human race. No wonder then that he writes of his hesitancy over speaking of God, his sense of unity with his humanist colleagues both in the assassination plot and in Tegel, his assertion that we must all live as if God were not.

Bonhoeffer's increasing uncertainty concerning the words and concepts of faith is not a sign of loss of faith, but rather of a renewed experience of faith. For the person undergoing this experience (and even more so for those looking on), it can seem at the time as if they are losing faith, as they become less and less certain of previously unquestioned aspects of belief. St Teresa of Avila pictures the experience as a cocoon. Tragically, Dietrich Bonhoeffer died before he had emerged from the cocoon, and so we are in the perplexing position of being able to see what he had lost, while merely glimpsing what was to be.

In the life of Dietrich Bonhoeffer, the contemplative experience manifests itself where we would not expect it to do so. Bonhoeffer stands as a reminder of the universality of the contemplative experience; once the human superstructure of our religious traditions is stripped away, the naked reality of all life and experience is none other than God.

During his time in Tegel prison, Bonhoeffer wrote a poem describing his inner struggles between the calmness and composure of his public persona, and the loneliness and yearning of his inner self. The poem ends with a question and an answer:

Who am I? This or the other?
Am I one person today, and tomorrow another?
Am I both at once? A hypocrite before others,
and before myself a contemptibly woebegone
    weakling?
Or is something within me still like a beaten army,
fleeing in disorder from victory already achieved?

Who am I? They mock me these lonely questions of
    mine.
Whoever I am, thou knowest, O God, I am thine.[25]

4

Etty Hillesum
'At One with All Existence'

Esther Hillesum was born on 15 January 1914 in Middelburg, Holland. Her parents sum up in their own selves the contrasting sides of Etty's personality as it comes through to us from her writings. Her father, we are told, was an excellent and disciplined scholar, while her mother was 'passionate, chaotic and in almost everything the opposite of her husband'.[1]

Both Etty and her two brothers, Mischa and Jaap, showed considerable ability at school. Mischa was apparently considered one of the most promising pianists in Europe, and Jaap became a doctor, but both tragically died in the horror and chaos of the Third Reich.

Etty left school in 1932, and went on to take a degree in law at the University of Amsterdam, before enrolling in the Faculty of Slavonic Languages. At the time her diaries start, she was living in Nazi-occupied Amsterdam and earning her living through private Russian language tuition. The owner of the house in which she lived, a 62 year-old widower named Hans Wegerif, had asked her to come and live there as a sort of housekeeper, but an intimate relationship soon developed.

The most significant person and influence on Etty's life during the months covered by the diaries was Julius

Spier. Spier was a practising psychochirologist (one who studies the science and psychology of palm prints), and Etty had a number of therapeutic sessions with him before becoming his assistant and, later, his intellectual partner and lover.

The diary starts in March 1941. Sixteen months later, Etty was given a job as typist in the Jewish Council in Amsterdam, an organization formed by the Nazis as an executive for the orders of the regime as they affected Jews. Those who worked for the council did so in the hope that they could help their fellow Jews. This turned out to be an illusion. Etty worked for the council for a mere fourteen days before she volunteered to accompany a group of Jewish prisoners to Westerbork transit camp. There she worked in the camp hospital, making periodic visits back to Amsterdam thanks to a council travel permit. In September 1943 she was taken with her parents and brother Mischa to Auschwitz. And it was there, on 30 November 1943, that she died.

It is out of the raw material of this life that the extraordinary spiritual power of Etty's diaries comes to us. Etty was, in all respects, a fully human person. She lived and loved and ate and loved again. We are not told of any formal religious affiliation. Certainly she does not record for us any attendance at religious worship. And yet here is the diary of a woman who articulates, and lives, a profoundly creative and powerful spirituality.

The first time I read Etty's diaries, in Amsterdam at the International Bonhoeffer Society Conference, I was struck by the common ground between the Jewish woman and the Christian pastor. That sense has not left me. I remain convinced that these diaries belong alongside the works of such figures as Dietrich Bonhoeffer and Thomas Merton as authentic expressions of a contemplative faith in our troubled times.

At One with the World

At the heart of the spirituality of Etty Hillesum is a profound awareness of what we might term 'connectedness'. Late in 1941, some eight months after commencing her diary, she describes 'a feeling of being at one with all existence'.

Later she describes her sense of connectedness as a oneness in time as well as in space: 'I am not alone in my tiredness or sickness or fears, but at one with millions of others from many centuries . . .'[2]

This was not just an abstract solidarity. It had implications, and the diary indicates that these implications were taken seriously. Solidarity means: 'I am in Poland every day, on the battlefields . . . I am with the hungry, with the ill-treated and the dying, every day.' But it also means that 'I am . . . with the jasmine and with that piece of sky beyond my window'.[3]

This solidarity means too a sense of oneness even with the enemy. A friend's experience with a kindly German soldier reminds Hillesum that even the enemy is human:

And when Liesl told me all this, I knew at once: I shall have to pray for this German soldier. Out of all those uniforms one has been given a face now. There will be other faces, too, in which we shall be able to read something we understand: that German soldiers suffer as well. There are no frontiers between suffering people, and we must pray for them all.[4]

It was this increasing sense of connectedness which led

Hillesum to her decision to go voluntarily with her fellow Jews to Westerbork. In September 1942, after a few weeks at the camp, she prayed: 'One day, I would love to travel through all the world, oh God; I feel drawn right across all frontiers and feel a bond with all Your warring creatures.' She then added the rider: 'But first I must be present on every battle-front and at the centre of all human suffering.'[5]

Back in Amsterdam, faced with the likelihood of exemption from return to Westerbork because of ill-health, Hillesum was deeply disappointed. For solidarity accepts no exemptions:

> I don't ever want to be what they call 'safe'. I want to be there [presumably she is referring to Westerbork]. I want to fraternise with all my so-called enemies, I want to understand what is happening and share my knowledge with as many as I can possibly reach . . .[6]

In the end she returned to Westerbork, and was eventually transported to Auschwitz. Her sense of connectedness and her solidarity with human suffering led Hillesum to the horror of her final destination.

'We must share our love with the whole of creation,'[7] she wrote. For: 'We *are* "at home". Under the sky. In every place on earth, if only we carry everything with us.'[8]

It is that 'everything' to which we now turn our attention.

At Home in the World

For Etty Hillesum, even in the midst of the horrors of Nazi occupation and their increasing stranglehold on the

Jews, life continued to have meaning and beauty. Time and time again she speaks of the beauty of life and the humanity of the enemy. In one of the entries early in 1942 she speaks of her 'enormous faith and gratitude that life should be so beautiful'.

In itself this is a powerful statement, but what follows makes it an even more profound expression of the underlying beauty of life. For as she wrote these words, Hillesum was due to appear before the Gestapo – presumably for registration. Yet, as she writes, it is this sense of the beauty of life that makes even that experience an 'historic moment'.[9]

Writing about her time in the Gestapo Hall, Hillesum says that the 'real import' of the experience was not that she was shouted at, 'but that I felt no indignation, rather a real compassion'.

> . . . despite all the suffering and injustice I cannot hate others. All the appalling things that happen are no mysterious threats from afar, but arise from fellow beings very close to us. That makes these happenings more familiar, then, and not so frightening.

What is frightening and horrific is not individuals but systems. In her analysis, Hillesum speaks of what we would now term 'structural evil', and yet she maintains that the reality of such evil does not deny the fundamental beauty of the world. 'The terrifying thing is that systems grow too big for men and hold them in a satanic grip, the builders no less than the victims of the system.'[10]

The tension between beauty and evil is present in every situation, but most acutely in contexts such as Nazi-occupied Amsterdam. Here, beauty is hard to discern, and even harder to celebrate, amidst the horrors of suffering and death. Robert McAffee Brown wrote some years ago:

> I conclude that concern for beauty is not a moral cop-out. It leads us firmly into the midst of all that is going on in our world. Where there is beauty apparent, we are to enjoy it; where there is beauty hidden, we are to unveil it; where there is beauty defaced, we are to restore it; where there is no beauty, we are to create it. All of which places us, too, in the arena where oppression occurs, where the oppressed congregate, and where we are called to be.[11]

This, surely, is what Etty Hillesum strives to do. Yet she is as aware as anyone of the dangers of celebrating life's beauty in the midst of oppression and death:

> I try to face up to Your world, God, not to escape from reality into beautiful dreams – though I believe that beautiful dreams can exist beside the most horrible reality – and I continue to praise Your creation, God, despite everything.[12]

Life is not just beautiful, it also has meaning. Comparing life at home in Amsterdam with life in Westerbork, Hillesum is unable to separate the two. For both are manifestations of life:

> Surrounded by my writers and poets and the flowers on my desk I loved life. And there among the barracks, full of hunted and persecuted people, I found confirmation of my love of life. Life in those draughty barracks was no other than life in this protected, peaceful room. Not for one moment was I cut off from the life I was said to have left behind. There was simply one great, meaningful whole.[13]

Somehow she was able to face all that life was likely to throw at her, in all its absurdity and pointlessness, and still claim that life is meaningful. However, her conviction that life is meaningful was one which she hardly dared articulate to others. Yet she had clearly 'looked our destruction, our miserable end which has already begun in so many small ways in our daily life, straight in the eye and accepted it into my life, and my love of life has not been diminished'.[14]

Indeed, what is important is not that the inevitable end be avoided, but that 'even as we die a terrible death we are able to feel right up to the very last moment that life has meaning and beauty, that we have realised our potential and lived a good life'.[15]

Again, this sense of life's beauty and meaning is not just an abstract feeling. It leads to a commitment to future generations, and hence to the present. Those who are yet to come need to know that life has meaning. And so it is for their sake as well as one's own that beauty, meaning and integrity are to be preserved:

> And that is why I must try to live a good and faithful life to my last breath: so that those who come after me do not have to start all over again, need not face the same difficulties. Isn't that doing something for future generations?[16]

In the end, Etty Hillesum could claim that life is beautiful because she believed in God. She records a conversation with a friend in which she, spontaneously and almost unawares, confesses her belief in God. This is how she can make such claims. And it is to the nature and implications of her belief in God that we now turn our attention.

'You See, I Believe in God.'

This simple, yet profound statement seems to surprise Etty Hillesum. To speak of God was more intimate for her than speaking of sex. To speak of God demanded courage. Some of this may be attributed to the traditional Jewish reluctance to utter the name of God, but probably more significant is the inappropriateness of using the word 'God' in face of such chaos and suffering. For how can one dare to speak of God when millions are dying, and the superstructure of faith and religion has been subverted for such horrific and blasphemous ends?

It is difficult for us to imagine just how unexpected and incongruous Hillesum's confession of faith in God would have sounded to many of her compatriots. Yet for her, belief in God was an increasingly important part of life.

Central to Hillesum's belief in God is a belief that human beings are dwellings for God. In an entry for July 1942 she writes of the importance of safeguarding 'that little piece of You, God, in ourselves. And perhaps in others as well'.[17] Some months later she is more certain of the importance of the latter: 'Every one must be turned into a dwelling dedicated to You, oh God. And I promise You . . . that I shall try to find a dwelling and a refuge for You in as many houses as possible.'[18]

For Hillesum, God is primarily to be found within God's creatures as the source of beauty, meaning and love. This is how she can claim that individuals remain objects of love despite the evil that they commit. This is also how she can speak of her connectedness with all creation, of being at home in every place. For where life is, there too is God.

Because of this, the task of the believer in God is to

42

help others to become aware of their connectedness with God and with each other. But first we must cultivate this connectedness in ourselves. Hillesum herself confesses: 'It truly is difficult to carry You intact with me and to remain faithful to You through everything, as I have always promised.'[19]

What then does it involve to live out this awesome truth that where life is, there is God? Most importantly, it is about simplicity and honesty. It is to rid ourselves 'of all preconceptions, of all slogans, of all sense of security, [to] find the courage to let go of everything, every standard, every conventional bulwark'.[20]

This means forgetting such words as 'God', 'death', 'suffering' and 'eternity', and instead to become 'as simple and as wordless as the growing corn or the falling rain. [To] . . . just be'.[21]

It is to listen both to ourselves and to others[22] – and hence to God – and to be utterly honest with ourselves and with God: 'Mysticism must rest on crystal-clear honesty, can only come after things have been stripped down to their naked reality.'[23]

Reading through Etty Hillesum's diaries, one is struck by the self-awareness of the writer. She writes early on in the diaries of her need to 'come to grips' with herself. In the course of the same entry she notes: 'I still lack a basic tune . . .'[24]

Some eight months later, Hillesum is able to discern that 'a thread does run through my life, through my reality, like a continuous line'.[25] Furthermore, she is convinced of the importance of consistency: 'Unless every smallest detail in your daily life is in harmony with the high ideals you profess, then those ideals have no meaning.'[26]

Like so many of us, Etty Hillesum found herself

struggling to keep up with her expanding awareness of both her own self and the needs of others. Early on in the diaries, she speaks of the need to change ourselves before we begin to change the world.[27] Yet even in Westerbork, where she had put her ideals into uncomfortable practice, she clearly feels there is a way to go:

> I keep talking about God the whole day long, and it is high time that I lived accordingly. I still have a long way to go . . . and yet sometimes I behave as if I were there already. I am frivolous and easy-going and I often look on things that happen as if I were an artist, a mere observer. There is something bizarre and fickle and adventurous in me. But as I sit here at my desk, late at night, I also feel a compelling directive voice deep down, a great and growing seriousness, a soundless voice that tells me what to do and forces me to confess: I have fallen short in all ways, my real work has not even begun. So far I have done little more than play about.[28]

A Framework For Faith

Etty Hillesum defies our attempts to label her. By upbringing she was Jewish. In conversation with a colleague, she is accused of advocating Christianity. Her response is typically spirited: 'I, amused by your confusion, retort quite coolly, "Yes, Christianity, and why ever not?"'[29]

Yet we must resist our impulse to label Etty Hillesum, to claim her for one or other of our religious camps. For her strength and her power are precisely in her universality.

What we can and must do, however, is to make

connections. Etty's spirituality and world-view are all about connectedness. If our world is indeed one connected whole, then our differing approaches to God are also part of that whole. Etty Hillesum's contribution to our reflections stands in its own right. But, more specifically, the clear parallels between her thought and that of others who stand self-consciously within the theological, religious and ecclesiastical parameters of Christianity tell us that there are certain insights and experiences which are common to all men and women of faith.[30]

Hillesum reminds us, yet again, of the universality of the contemplative experience. Once the illusions are stripped away, the naked reality of all existence is none other than God. Or, in Hillesum's own words:

> On the whole, a person more or less contemplative by nature isn't suited to describing a specific place or event. One discovers that the basic materials of life are the same everywhere, and that one can live one's life with meaning - or else one can die - in any spot on this earth.[31]

5

A New Way of Seeing
Contemplation and Connectedness

> In our day, the personal crisis of faith for the individual has
> become the corporate crisis of faith for the Church, indeed
> the world, as a whole. In this century of Auschwitz,
> Hiroshima, the Ozone Layer, and so much else, the 'Dark
> Night' is no longer the experience of the few. For many in our
> day the traditional words have indeed broken down, and new
> images are sorely needed.[1]

We live in a time of ferment. Previously accepted concepts, boundaries and norms in the social, political and
economic fields have proved to be dispensable. The
superpower mentality of the Cold War has been
replaced by new forms of tribalism.[2] The ideologies of
both communism and capitalism have proved wanting,
and both political right and left are engaged in a redef-
inition of their positions. In religion, the established
Churches of the developed northern hemisphere are
losing both influence and adherents, while the new
Churches of both north and south, as well as the prolif-
erating new religious movements, are gaining ground.

Ferment – or impasse? For many, the loss of established certainties is cause for concern. Not least in the
Churches the question is being asked: 'Where will it all
end?' Yet in the Church's own contemplative tradition
the experience of impasse is in fact a time of opportunity,

a stimulus to action, an invitation to seek and discover new ways of expressing and embodying the insights and values of the Christian community. As old words, concepts and structures break down, we are freed to confess their constraining influence and to explore and experiment with new and liberating ones!

This, to a certain extent, is precisely what is happening both in politics and religion. Of course, there are two ways of approaching an impasse. One is to accept it as a *kairos* – a time of new opportunity. The other is to deny it and to entrench oneself in the words and structures of the past. The first of these two responses is exemplified in the lives and thought of our three subjects.

Merton the Contemplative

For Thomas Merton, as we have seen, the word 'contemplation' describes a process by which one discovers the reality of God, oneself and the world. The presupposition of this process is a sense of the inadequacy of human verbalizations and embodiments of the divine. This was a characteristic of Merton from his early years, perhaps in part due to the unsettled, rootless nature of his childhood.

Even as early as his time at Columbia, Merton was described by one of his professors, Dan Walsh, as 'essentially Augustinian'. 'My bent was not so much toward the intellectual, dialectical, speculative character of Thomism, as toward the spiritual, mystical, voluntaristic and practical way of St Augustine and his followers.'[3]

This characteristic had certainly returned to the fore by the late 1950s, as Merton established his monastic identity and developed from a conventional to an individuative form of faith.[4] William Shannon notes that from this time on, Merton placed more trust in his own experience and exercised less caution in using poetic language to express it.[5] Merton's formative realization that no idea, image or concept could capture God emerged again as a central and controlling theme of his thought.

The contemplative is someone who has taken on board 'a new way of seeing'[6] and who therefore lives in a state of dis-illusionment. To be dis-illusioned, in the sense which Merton intends, is to discover the reality behind the illusions which dominate and preoccupy our world. To be dis-illusioned is, through a radical openness to the divine presence in all things, to have discovered God as the ultimate ground and reality of all that is. The contemplative way, therefore, can be said to be a journey of discovery in relation to three fundamental human questions.

Who is God? Central to the contemplative way is the simple yet profound insight that the nearer we get to God, the less we see. For the images and concepts with which we seek to grasp God are ultimately misleading. As Merton says: 'If nothing that can be seen can either be God or represent Him to us as He is, then to find God we must pass beyond everything that can be seen and enter into darkness.'

Therefore, to grow in one's relationship with God is to pass from light into darkness, from certainty to uncertainty. Words, images and concepts fall away as our illusions about God give way to the reality of God. The less we can – and want to – say about God, the better we know God: 'Faith terminates not in a statement, not in a formula of words, but *in God* . . . The importance of the formulas is not that they are ends in themselves, but that they are means through which God communicates His truth to us.'[7]

Who am I? No less important to the contemplative way as interpreted by Merton is the discovery of my own true identity. Any discovery of the reality of God implies a parallel discovery of my own reality. This is a twofold process, involving death and new life. It is death to the false self, rooted in a denial of the reality and claim of God, and therefore rooted in illusion. It is birth to the new self, rooted in the reality of God, myself, and each human being as a unique creation of God. For my identity cannot be discovered or established without reference to the wider human community of which I am a part. In our very diversity as unique persons lies also our unity as God's creation. In Merton's own words: 'I will never be able to find myself if I isolate myself from the rest of mankind as if I were a different kind of being.'[8]

What is real? The third question posed by Merton in his life and work is a question asked about the world at large: what is real? If contemplation is all about a new way of seeing, and if this leads to the stripping away of illusions about God and my own self, then the contemplative must inevitably see the world in a new way.

In contrast to some religious traditions, the contemplative's attitude toward the world is profoundly affirmative. He or she is concerned not with rejection of and retreat from the world, but rather with experiencing the world with a clarity not easily possible for those in the thick of it. In the words of John Garvey: 'We ordinarily think of monks as people who flee what we call "the real world" rather than people who are passionate about encountering reality with a clarity which the world tends to obscure.'[9]

That Merton was graced with such a clarity of observation and perception can be seen in many of his writings from the 1960s. He draws parallels between the mentality of the Nazi era and that of his own time, points to what he regards as 'pseudo events' and predicts – controversially at the time, yet accurately as it turned out – a coming racial explosion.[10]

The contemplative way is all about a greater and more intimate knowledge of and engagement with reality, God, the self and the world. The journey towards the reality of one is of necessity a journey towards the reality of all, for all are connected. Merton's journey along the contemplative way led to the discovery that God was to be found in movements for peace and justice, as well as in non-Christian religions, for just as words cannot capture God, nor too can our human institutions, structures and boundaries. As Christopher Nugent puts it: 'Everything that *deepens* tends to converge.'[11]

This explains our discovery in this book that figures as diverse as Merton the Catholic monk, Bonhoeffer the Lutheran pastor and Etty Hillesum the non-practising Jew can in fact be found together traversing the contemplative way.

Bonhoeffer the Contemplative

Throughout his life, Dietrich Bonhoeffer identified himself with the Lutheran Protestant tradition. And yet, during his time in prison, Bonhoeffer demonstrated signs of undergoing an experience similar to that described by John of the Cross as the dark night of the soul. We are in a position to identify a connection that Bonhoeffer himself could not be expected to make. Furthermore, it appears that Bonhoeffer's dark night can most effectively be understood by considering him as a contemplative – as one who, like Merton, sought the reality of God, his own personhood and the world.

At first, this sounds both an inappropriate and an incongruous description of one who was so thoroughly Lutheran in his theology and devotion. Yet, on reflection, it makes sense, because the terminology of illusion and reality appropriately describes the shifts of Bonhoeffer's final years.

The unmasking of the illusion of certainty has begun already in Bonhoeffer's *The Cost of Discipleship*. Here, despite his forceful call to discipleship, he noticeably refuses to offer specific shape to that call. Discipleship is not a call to a specific course of action decided in advance, but a call to follow Jesus Christ.

Some years later, in the various writings which make up the *Ethics*, Bonhoeffer displays this same hesitancy to codify ethical options in advance. However, here the focus has shifted from Jesus Christ as he is met in the gospel story to Jesus Christ as he is met in the specific situation and, more precisely, in the neighbour. He is 'the origin, essence and goal of all that is real', and so 'action that is in accordance with Christ is action that is in accordance with reality'.[12]

In practice, this means that for Bonhoeffer:

> The responsible man is dependent on the man who is concretely his neighbor in his concrete possibility. His conduct is not established in advance, once and for all . . . as a matter of principle, but it arises with the given situation. He has no principle at his disposal which possesses absolute validity . . . he perceives that the 'absolute good' may sometimes be the very worst.[13]

Elsewhere in the *Ethics*, Bonhoeffer notes that much of

life is concerned with the 'self evident' – those times when 'the moral course goes without saying'. At most points in our lives there is no moral or ethical problem to be solved; merely life to be lived. Here we are no different from the rest of humanity, struggling to respond in a responsible way to each given situation. And it is precisely in that responsible living that, for the Christian, Jesus Christ is to be found.

Bonhoeffer also shows us that there is no certainty in our verbal expressions of faith. The experience of the German people under Nazism led him to make his well known claim that there was effectively a moratorium on words in the Church of his time and place.[14] Words both express and constitute certainty. When words lose their force and become redundant, their very redundancy is both the cause and result of a loss of certainty. For behind the crisis of intelligibility facing the Church lies the fact that in society at large belief in God has been judged irrelevant and discarded. This, of course, was clearly exemplified in the philosophy and practice of Nazism, where God was effectively replaced by fuehrer and Reich.

As certainties about the content and shape of religious belief become less clear, so too does any conception of what it means to be religious. Bonhoeffer identified many of his compatriots in the conspiracy as 'unconscious' – and no doubt also 'religionless' – Christians. By the end of his life, it appears that his conception of what it means to be a Christian had become much more inclusive and open-ended. This is intriguing in the light of his strongly exclusive warnings against the so-called 'German Christians' at the time of the formation of the Confessing Church.[15] With the traditional signs of religious belief at best unreliable, other criteria now had to be utilized:

'responsible action', true humanity, class and culture.

The unmasking of the illusion of innocence was an important experience for Bonhoeffer. Coming as he did from an upper middle class family, sheltered for much of his life from the harsh realities of the wider world, the rise of Nazism shattered his youthful illusions. His class had failed their nation – they had allowed Hitler and the Nazis to gain power. There were no innocent bystanders.

Thus Bonhoeffer could write in the *Ethics* that the Church is 'the fellowship of the confession of guilt', accepting the burden of its own guilt, and also the guilt of the 'western world' as it exists without reference to Jesus Christ.[16] It is impossible to read these words without recalling the biographical situation in which they were written. The writer was only too aware of his own guilt, his own share in the responsibility of his class for allowing Hitler to take hold. Yet the Church, by contrast, seemed strangely reluctant publicly to confess its guilt or to act on it. As Bonhoeffer wrote:

> If any man tries to escape guilt in responsibility . . . he sets his own personal innocence above his respon-sibility for men, and he is blind to the more irre-deemable guilt which he incurs precisely in this; he is blind also to the fact that real innocence shows itself precisely in a man's entering into the fellowship of guilt for the sake of other men.[17]

The 'ultimate question', therefore, does not concern the preservation of one's own moral innocence, nor is it concerned with the preservation of one's own life, but rather it asks 'how the coming generation is to live'.[18] There are indeed no such persons as innocent by-standers. All share in 'the fellowship of human guilt', and so I am guilty before I say or do anything: guilty precisely because I am a member of the human race; guilty because I am inescapably part of a particular time and place, with all its joys and sorrows, successes and failures, loves and hates.

This helps us to understand how Bonhoeffer could enter so wholeheartedly into the moral ambiguity of the double life of an Abwehr agent and anti-Nazi conspirator. That his position involved very real guilt is revealed in the recent disclosure that Bonhoeffer's work with the Abwehr very probably led to the death of a small number of Jews. Yet in Bonhoeffer's terms, the question must be asked as to the price of *not* taking on the double life which led – directly through his Abwehr work – to their death. The innocence he would have gained would have been merely an illusion, for it would have been the product of an evasion of responsibility, itself an even more 'irredeemable guilt'. It should be said that Bonhoeffer's double-edged work with the Abwehr also led to a number of Jews being saved.

The illusion of separation is, in a sense, the reverse side of the illusion of innocence. It was Bonhoeffer's increasing sense of solidarity with his fellow human beings which led him to reflect on the sense of separation which characterized so many of his class. His *Fiction from Prison* is preoccupied with reflections on class. Both drama and novel indicate Bonhoeffer's own unease, no doubt experienced in Tegel, with his own distance from the lives and experiences of ordinary people, and his own ambivalent attitude concerning their place in society.

It appears that Bonhoeffer never succeeded in reconciling his conviction that society needed an elite with the New Testament conviction that in Jesus Christ all ultimate distinctions of class or culture have been removed. In his novel we find a reflection on what must have been the two conflicting instincts in Bonhoeffer's own mind. Two boys – no doubt representing Bonhoeffer's own upbringing and basic instincts – recall St Paul's conviction that 'all people are supposed to be equal', and later add: 'That's the exact opposite, after all, of what both of us experience and think and want every day.'

Then they ask themselves what Frau Brake – the undoubted voice of Bonhoeffer's own Christian conscience – would say to their dilemma, and answer their own question by articulating their hope that she would surely agree with them.[19] In the fiction the dilemma is not resolved. Nor does it appear ever to have been resolved in Bonhoeffer's own mind.

Yet if he could not quite accept the notion that society could be governed without a ruling elite, Bonhoeffer certainly awoke to the reality of human solidarity. As he wrote: 'We have for once learnt to see the great events of world history from below . . . from the perspective of those who suffer.'[20]

For Bonhoeffer, human solidarity is grounded in God's solidarity with humanity in Jesus Christ. The perspective of those who suffer is precisely the perspective in which the world is seen through the eyes of Jesus Christ – the suffering God. For this reason, the view from below is a profoundly Christian perspective, and marks for Bonhoeffer the unmasking of the illusion of separation.

A final manifestation of his growing sense of solidarity with the whole of humanity – outside his own class and Christian faith – can be found in Bonhoeffer's conviction that 'before God and with God we live without God'. This is perhaps the ultimate expression of solidarity that a Christian can make. That we live, by God's own intention, as those 'who would manage their lives without him'.[21]

Within a year of penning those words, Dietrich Bonhoeffer was dead. In his death, as in his life, he sought no privileges because of his class or faith. He died a death shared by many millions of God's children during the horrific years of the Reich. Here, like the Christ he followed, was solidarity even unto death.

Bonhoeffer's personal, social and theological experience in Tegel prison is captured in the words of Constance Fitzgerald in her essay on St John's dark night for today:

> At the deepest levels of night, in a way one could not have imagined it could happen, one sees the withdrawal of all one has been certain of and depended upon for reassurance and affirmation . . . support systems that give life meaning: concepts, systems of meaning, symbolic structures, relationships, institutions.[22]

Bonhoeffer the contemplative surely knew Fitzgerald's 'emptiness, confusion, isolation, weakness, abandonment'. Indeed, it can be argued that he knew these in a more profound way even than St John, for he knew them not just on a personal and spiritual level, but on a social and political level too. It was not just the individual who had entered the dark night; it was a whole society, culture and people.

Increasingly, Bonhoeffer became aware of the inadequacy of many of the traditional expressions of Christian faith, both to his life as an Abwehr agent and anti-Hitler conspirator, and also to his fellow conspirators and, later, fellow prisoners in Tegel. This experience, coupled with his own temperamental hesitancy to speak of God – especially to those who did not share his belief – led to the increasingly intuitive and open-ended theology of his final years.

Politically and ecclesiastically, too, Bonhoeffer found himself in an intensely difficult situation. The concepts of Christianity were being misused, as the 'German Christians' adopted the fuehrer and the Third Reich as the personification of Christ and his kingdom; its values were being rejected, as seen in the persecution of the Jews and other expressions of blind intolerance; and its structures were being inverted, as in the Confessing Church, whose primary concern was to preserve its own doctrinal and confessional purity.

Together, these three aspects of Bonhoeffer's situation amounted to a total impasse, where new and creative ways of being, thinking and doing as a Christian were certainly called for.

Hillesum the Contemplative

Faced with the 'massive public suffering'[23] of our century, it is tempting to reject beauty as a theological category of the privileged, irrelevant to the situation of the vast majority of creatures on the planet. Yet this was not so for Etty Hillesum. She refused to deny the presence and importance of beauty even in the midst of the pain and brokenness of an occupied country, where she and her fellow Jews were becoming increasingly marginalized.

It is precisely in her concern to find the good, the true and the beautiful, even in the midst of the pain and evil which she chronicles in her diaries, that we engage profoundly with her most significant contribution to our exploration. Etty Hillesum was a person who made connections, and one of these is the connection between beauty and humiliation.

The writer and philosopher Albert Camus spoke of the need to do justice to both beauty and the humiliated, and that call remains as relevant to our own time as it was for his. Indeed, in our own time, such theological and spiritual currents as creation spirituality serve to remind us of the dangers of too pessimistic a view of reality. There is a sense in which pessimism can become a self-fulfilling prophecy: we expect to see evil and therefore we fail to look for the good and the beautiful. To deny the fundamental beauty and blessedness of our world is ultimately to deny the possibility of goodness – or at least to devalue it – and to accept evil as inevitable, and one's attitude towards it as one of resigned pessimism.

The wholistic view of life and reality which characterizes the contemplative can be found in Etty Hillesum. Despite the horrors of the occupation of her own country, and the Nazi expansion throughout Europe, and despite the ever-tightening noose of persecution around the necks of her own people, Hillesum refuses to give up on the world. She refuses to deny that beauty can and does still exist even in the midst of unspeakable fear and horror.

Again, her conviction is all about illusion and reality. For Hillesum, it was imperative 'to be there right in the thick of what people call "horror" and still be able to say: life is beautiful'.[24] To do otherwise would have given evil the last word, admitting that beauty and meaning are but wistful illusions. In fact, as Hillesum is so obviously convinced, both beauty and humiliation are real. Yet in the time of suffering or crisis it is all too easy to attribute ultimate reality to evil. This Etty Hillesum refuses to do.

Instead, she disarms evil not by denying its existence – which would be naive and foolish – but by denying its power ultimately to define what life is all about. In this way she seeks to dis-illusion herself and others from the notion that God's creation is fundamentally evil. In her own words, it is about seeing through to the reality behind every human evil, that 'no one is really "bad" deep down'.[25]

In her awareness of the structural nature of evil, Hillesum successfully separates the evil of human created systems of oppression, such as Nazism, from the individuals who are implicated in them. In this way she can dare to love her enemies, affirming their common humanity and praying for their welfare.

Hillesum saw that our description of others as 'evil' or 'bad', with all its implications, is nothing other than a way of sidestepping our own evil and guilt. Rather than hating others, therefore, we should be working on that which others hate in ourselves and thus realizing our common humanity and shared struggle between good and evil. Indeed, when we look into our own lives we find 'so much work to do on ourselves' that hatred of our enemies becomes impossible.

It is remarkable how little Etty Hillesum seeks answers or makes judgements in her writings. Her major concern appears to be the making of connections – that, Jew or Nazi, we share a common humanity, a common guilt, and even a common capacity for beauty. Hers too is the intuitive, connecting spirituality which characterizes the contemplative way, and yet which is also so much at one with the experience of us all.

Connectedness and Universality

Etty Hillesum's affirmation of the beauty and meaning of creation is echoed in a letter of Thomas Merton to a young correspondent. He affirms that while 'the world in itself can never be evil', nevertheless, human power, greed and domination can lead to it becoming 'in some sense the victim of their greed and [taking on] the character of those who make use of it in a sinful way'.[26]

Like Hillesum, Merton is at pains to affirm the goodness and blessedness of creation – presumably including human beings – while also admitting the existence and very real presence of evil. However, the world 'in itself' – again, presumably including human beings – remains God's good creation. As James Carpenter has observed: 'The things that make life endurable and sometimes even enjoyable have a legitimate place in a responsible theology. They help to give substance to the affirmation that creation is good . . .'[27]

Bonhoeffer's image of love for God as a *cantus firmus* (ground-base or consistent theme), to which the various melodies of life unfold in counterpoint, stands alongside Hillesum's notion that the fundamental reality of beauty and love cannot be denied by the existence, and even the prevalence, of evil and hatred. Both bring to us what contemplatives call the 'still centre' – the point at which we are one with all reality, and from which we face and live life not as it pretends to be but as it really is.

That still centre is common to all expressions of religious faith – and even beyond, as our three subjects themselves testify. On his last journey to the East, Merton spoke of 'the importance of serious communication, and indeed of "communion", among contemplatives of different traditions, disciplines, and religions'. Such communion is 'beyond the level of words, a communion in authentic experience which is shared not only on a "preverbal" level but also on a "postverbal" level'.[28]

In a very different way, Bonhoeffer struggled to come to terms with the fact that so many of his fellow Christians were able to accept the Nazi regime, with all its horrors, while members of his family who had never professed any form of religious belief seemed to exhibit a more authentically Christian response to the events going on around them. Among his unfinished notes from prison we read: 'Unconscious Christianity: the left hand does not know what the right hand is doing. Matt. 25.'[29] This New Testament reference is to Jesus' parable of the sheep and the goats, where individuals are commended for serving a God they neither recognized nor expected.[30]

In all three of our subjects we find a sense of connectedness which the psychologist James Fowler refers to as characterizing the ultimate stage of faith development: universalizing faith. Walter Conn describes this as going 'beyond the paradoxical balancing of "opposites" by transcending all dichotomies in identifying with all, including the transcendent, in a community of universal inclusiveness, of Being'.[31]

At this culminating stage of religious development, 'Full self-realization . . . is found in full self-transcendence.'[32]

In other words, all is one, and the ultimate fulfilment of my own identity is found as I become aware that I am not the independent 'I' which I appear to be, but rather a dependent 'I', part of the greater whole.

The contemplative's 'still point' is similar in function to the Quaker's 'inner light', or 'divine spark'. It is the point at which each of us is at one with the greater whole

- with God and with one another. Or, expressed as the metaphor that it is, it is a reminder of our connectedness. Charlene Spretnak describes such experiences as 'states of grace', and calls for them to be nurtured and respected:

> When we experience consciousness of the unity in which we are embedded, the sacred whole that is in and around us, we exist in a state of grace. At such moments our consciousness perceives not only our individual self, but also our larger self, the self of the cosmos.[33]

> Experiencing grace is only one aspect of spiritual practice, but it is particularly important for a culture that has validated only perceptions of separateness and fragmentation.[34]

Fundamental to the contemplative way is a sense of connectedness, wholeness and integration. These are characteristics of the legacy of Thomas Merton, Dietrich Bonhoeffer and Etty Hillesum. But they are also the concerns of others too. In our final chapter we will consider what has been referred to as theology's 'new paradigm', and ask how it helps us to speak of God and reality in this time of impasse and opportunity.

A New Way of Doing Theology
The 'New Paradigm'

One can assign Merton and Bonhoeffer similar functions in the process of cultural transition. Twenty-five years before Merton's death, Bonhoeffer proclaimed a 'humankind come of age'. Merton was on to something similar, it seemed, though the stakes could no longer be restricted to European civilisation, but focused on the rapprochement between Eastern and Western cultures. Furthermore, it is intriguing that Merton, like Bonhoeffer in his *Letters and Papers from Prison*, was in touch with considerations whose greater manifestation occurred after his death. In specific ways, both had been able to sketch the configuration of a portion of the future before the future had broken through.[1]

There is a tendency in the works of our precursors . . . to discuss the Christian faith without any intensive attention to the particularities under which the discussion is taking place . . . It is even typical of them that they (politely?) avoid sharing with their readers the specifics of their own existence . . . [and even their sense of place].[2]

The last thirty years have seen enormous changes in the theological landscape, too. Theology has become self-conscious of its context, its concerns and the auto-biographical factors in its shape and form. These considerations are now seen to matter, making a difference to the type of theology which will emerge.

Therefore, theology differs according to its place (the *favelas* of Latin America, or the academies of Europe or North America); the race and gender of its practitioners (feminist, black, Afro-Caribbean); the central motifs and concerns of its project (liberation and political theologies, creation theology); and its cultural and spiritual roots (Korean, Japanese, South African).

Faced with these changes, and aware of similar changes in science, politics and culture, many commentators have spoken of a 'paradigm shift' in theology. The term 'paradigm' is originally a scientific term, coined by Thomas Kuhn to refer to what he described as 'an entire constellation of beliefs, values, techniques, and so on shared by the members of a given community'.[3]

In relation to theology, Hans Kung suggests the language of models, with a paradigm defined as an 'interpretive model', or as 'models for understanding'.[4] However we define a paradigm, the suggestion is that the basic theological model – not just the *what* but the *how* – with which we have interpreted the world around us since the Enlightenment has now reached breaking point. To use biblical imagery, we need new wineskins to contain the new wine of spiritual reality, here and now in the century of Auschwitz and Hiroshima. In other words, for many theologians the discipline of theology has reached an impasse.

Perhaps the most comprehensive study of paradigm theory in relation to theology is the collection of papers edited by Hans Kung and David Tracy under the title *Paradigm Change in Theology*.

The situation faced by religion in our time is put into focus by Edward Schillebeeckz in his paper, 'The Role of History in What is Called the New Paradigm'. He describes the tension between a transcendent and trans-cultural gospel and its embodiment and expression in the forms of a specific culture: 'Only in the concrete and in the particular can the gospel be the revelation of the universality of God and his salvation.'[5]

The problem, of course, is posed by radical changes – 'epochal ruptures', as Schillebeeckz calls them – in the prevailing culture. Other contributors to the symposium suggest characteristics of our present 'rupture', which include increasing pluralism within society, religion in general, and in Christianity itself.[6] Paradoxically, there is also an increasing awareness of the common ground between the different Christian traditions. Alongside these changes there is also a shift from a mechanistic worldview of domination to a more wholistic and inter-dependent one,[7] and a general weakening and loss of influence of western culture.[8]

The nature of the impasse faced by theology is clear. Much theology and Christian practice in the West is rooted in a worldview characterized by dominance – north over south, Church over world, uniformity over diversity. The newly-emerging values of pluralism, inter-dependence and openness present a very different cultural context. Many of the forms of embodiment and expression previously used by theology have now lost their ability to function as channels for the communication of God's love in word and deed.

To put it another way: 'an entire constellation of beliefs, values, techniques' – that is, a 'paradigm' – is being called into question and replaced by an alternative set. If this is true of a culture, it must also become true for the religion of that culture; otherwise it will lapse into irrelevance, caught in the thought forms of a different age.

Like other disciplines, theology too is invited to reflect on its own new paradigm, as it ponders, like Merton, Bonhoeffer and Hillesum, on what it means to believe in God in this age of Auschwitz, Hiroshima and environmental devastation.

Kung and Tracy's symposium makes two tentative suggestions in defining the characteristic of theology's new paradigm. Schillebeeckz suggests the paradigm of humanity. He observes: 'A religion which in fact has a dehumanizing effect, in whatever way, is either a false religion or a religion which understands itself wrongly.'[9] Johann Baptist Metz, by contrast, suggests the term 'liberation', contrasting it with the Reformation concern with liberty.[10]

A number of theologians have attempted to discern and explore the trajectories of the new paradigm. We shall look briefly at three of them.

Larry Rasmussen

What are the characteristics of a theology for our time? In an article first published in 1988, Larry Rasmussen observed that something is afoot in theology: '"Consensus" is premature, and not quite the word, but shared dynamics and converging themes are visible.'[11]

One embodiment of these shared dynamics can be found in the rise of religions of the marginalized. The second, and more relevant to our concerns here, is what Rasmussen refers to as 'the conceptual and ritual revisioning of inherited traditions in times of deep, often bewildering, change'.[12]

Common to these two movements are a number of themes. First, there has been a movement away from a theology of universal application and validity, towards theology as 'a communal process from a self-consciously defined and particular perspective'.[13] This means that we are faced with a variety of theologies, each rooted in their respective contexts, and therefore in the experience and identity of those who do the theologizing. In this way, 'reflection on shared experience' seeks to 'grasp existence theologically and socially in the same moment'.[14] This is fundamental to the new paradigm.

Second, Rasmussen sees a shift in the focus of theology from a concern primarily for the individual, to a concern also for public events and social systems. In face of the 'massive public suffering' of our century, the 'suffering and hidden God comes more and more to the fore'.[15]

Third, there has been a shift in the function of religion from consolation to transformation.

Fourth is a shift from what Rasmussen calls a Christocentric theology to a theocentric Christology; in other words, an increasing awareness that 'God, not Jesus, is the power at the centre of things, and a God-centred life is precisely what we see in Jesus'.[16]

This 'revisioning of inherited traditions' and concepts is precisely what St John's dark night is all about. It is interesting to note that theology, too, appears to be coming round to the mystics' insight that Jesus is not an end in himself, but rather the way to the end of all things, which is God. For St Teresa, this realization was a source of pain, and her expression of it in the form of a prayer to Jesus is both powerful and plaintive: 'Is it possible, my Lord, that for so much as an hour I could have entertained the thought that Thou couldst hinder my greatest good?'[17]

Rebecca Chopp

One of the works referred to by Larry Rasmussen in his article is Rebecca Chopp's *The Praxis of Suffering*, published in 1986. Chopp is concerned with two streams of theological reflection which have arisen largely since the late 1960s: liberation theology and political theology.

Chopp notes that both streams seek, in their language and witness, to embody the unity of 'faith and world', because the two can no longer be considered as 'separate realms'.[18] Liberation theology, in particular, unites creation and redemption – and thus also faith and world – in the promise of historical fulfilment, and so seeks to avoid much of the unhelpful dualism of the past.

Yet liberation theologians such as Jose Miguez Bonino are concerned to avoid extremes of either monism or dualism. For them it is therefore necessary to see all history – both the kingdom and concrete human history – as interrelated, but distinct. In such a view of history, the Church is seen as a sacrament of God's action in history. The action of God, embodied in the Church, is fundamentally a thrust towards liberation: 'God acting in history through human activity for the coming kingdom'.[19] In Chopp's words, this constitutes 'a new interpretation of the Christian faith, combining spirituality and politics . . .'[20] The two are inseparable: politics and spirituality are not separate realms but parts of one whole.

In the new paradigm, therefore, the content and concerns of theological reflection will be seen in a new light. Comparing the work of liberationist Gustavo Gutierrez with a work such as St Augustine's *Confessions*, Chopp writes of the latter as 'a theological journey on the historical path of faith . . .' And of both, she writes that they use theology as 'part of the process of a journey to God . . . which is, at the same time, a process of history, an active contemplation both in and of time'.[21]

Chopp indicates by her comparison of Augustine and Gutierrez that the latter's concern 'is not the "unpacking" of theological method but the weaving together of lived experience'.[22] She therefore suggests that the common genre of Augustine's *Confessions* and the work of Gutierrez is that of systematic theology. This is certainly a new way of looking at dogmatics! No more can the self be kept out of theology. From now on, the doer of theology has to identify herself and own up to her presuppositions of sex, race, culture, class and politics, any or all of which she brings to the theological project.

Chung Hyun-Kyung

In February 1991, an assembly of the World Council of Churches met in Canberra, Australia. One of the main speakers was a professor of theology from Seoul, Chung Hyun-Kyung. Her address was welcomed by some and condemned by others. It was variously described as syncretism, fatal pluralism, and acceptable diversity.[23]

At the centre of Chung's address was a call to repentance, a call to three urgent changes. The first change is from 'anthropocentrism' to 'life centrism': 'changing our center from human beings to all living beings has become our responsibility in order to survive'.[24]

The second change is from 'the habit of dualism' to 'the habit of interconnection':

> Our body and our spirit, our emotion and our mind, our world and God, immanence and transcendence, women and men, black and white, poor and rich: in

69

this culture we are divided against ourselves. We forget that we all come from the same source of life, God, and all the webs of our lives are interconnected.[25]

The third change is from 'the culture of death' to 'the culture of life'. At the same time that Chung delivered her address, thousands of miles away the Gulf War was being fought. This fact made one of her statements all the more poignant: 'Only when we can suffer with others (compassion) can we transform the culture of death to the culture of life . . .'[26]

Chung's address very powerfully expresses the feminist awareness of solidarity and connectedness, and presents it as a challenge for us all to take up. She concludes with an invitation:

> Let us tear apart all walls of division and the culture of death which separate us. And let us participate in the Holy Spirit's political economy of life, fighting for our life on this earth in solidarity with all living beings and building communities for justice, peace and the integrity of creation.[27]

Contemplatives and the New Paradigm

It is clear that something is afoot in theology. Theologians Larry Rasmussen, Rebecca Chopp and Chung Hyun-Kyung represent just three of many who could have been cited as explorers and explicators of that something we have referred to broadly as the new paradigm.[28]

Theology's new paradigm cannot be described as a new movement in theology, or a new school of theology, as much as a convergence or a common shift, noticed in

many varied and differing manifestations. It would
therefore be incorrect to speak of women and men delib-
erately starting to do theology in a new way. Instead, we
are witnessing people of both sexes and widely differing
cultures and concerns all doing theology in a way that
connects with one another – *even if they are not necessarily aware of the wider implications of what they are doing at
the time.*

Despite this diversity, there are a number of general
characteristics of theologies of the new paradigm. Four
of these are summarized below.

First, there has been a shift in the way theology is
done. Where once universals were applied irrespective of
context, theologians now recognize the importance of
context in defining the meaning, forms of expression
and embodiment of theology in a given situation. An
example of this is the way in which many theologians of
our time identify themselves and locate their place in the
Christian community – not just incidentally, but as a fundamental preparation for their theological enterprise.[29]

Second, there has been a shift in the content of
theology. The norm of scholastic objectivity has had to
make room for the experiential and intuitive: story,
poetry and connection-making. Matthew Fox is an
example of someone who embodies this methodology –
perhaps at times to excess.

Third, there has been a shift in the function of theology. Theology has changed from being an exploration
of meaning to become an agent of transformation. A
century after Marx condemned the philosophers for
seeking to understand the world rather than change it,
the theologians too are heeding his words. This is hardly surprising, given the increasing importance attributed

to the context of the one doing theology. After all, doing theology in Latin America without taking account of the poverty of its people is hardly doing theology at all!

Fourth, there has been a shift in the role of the theologian. The guardians of revealed truth have given way to the explorers of the human-divine project. In other words, Christian theology, in coming to terms with the existence of other religious traditions, is coming to see its role as articulating one among many ways to the one God. For the Christian explorer, Jesus is not so much our destination as our companion on the common human journey towards God.

We can see, therefore, that theology is emerging from its own dark night with a new agenda and a new methodology. It is emerging with a renewed sense of wholeness, connectedness and universality – and yet it is also intensely aware of the importance of context and rootedness for any meaningful conversation about the divine. It is emerging with a renewed sense of its vocation to help all who seek to discover and discern the presence of God in our interconnected world.

It is impossible to discern the contribution of Merton, Bonhoeffer and Hillesum to the shape and content of the new paradigm currently emerging. But what is clear is that they share a common perception of the nature, role and place of conversation about God and the self which is now shared by many theologians in our own time. Together with other representatives of the contemplative way, they recognize the importance of context, intuition and an awareness of the limits of language.

The experience of impasse has indeed turned out to be a *kairos* – calling us into new and long-neglected ways of expressing and embodying our faith in God. How we respond in our own time and place to the *kairos* we ourselves face, we cannot learn directly from our three subjects. For if their life and work show us anything, it is that real theology is always done in context. Yet from them we can glimpse what it might mean, and receive the challenge to work it out for our own lives.

Notes

We are grateful for permission to quote from the works cited below. Whilst every effort has been made to trace copyright owners, any oversights will be corrected in future editions.

CHAPTER 1
Impasse or Kairos?

1   Charlene Spretnak, *States of Grace: the Recovery of Meaning in the Post-Modern Age*. San Francisco: Harper-Collins, 1991, p. 224. © 1991 by Charlene Spretnak.

2   See Thomas C. Oden, *Two Worlds: Notes on the Death of Modernity in America and Russia*. Downers Grove: Inter-Varsity Press, 1992, pp. 33–36.

3   William Hamilton, *A Quest for the Post-Historical Jesus*. London: SCM Press/New York: Crossroad, 1993, p. 13 (SCM edn). Reprinted with permission from SCM Press.

4   John of the Cross, 'The Ascent of Mount Carmel' in *The Collected Works of St John of the Cross*. Washington DC: Institute of Carmelite Studies, 1979, p. 117. From *The Collected Works of St John of the Cross*, translated by Kieran Kavanaugh and Otilio Rodriguez. Copyright © 1979, 1991 by Washington Province of Discalced Carmelites. I.C.S. Publications, 2131 Lincoln Road N.E., Washington, DC 20002, USA.

5   John of the Cross, *Collected Works*, p. 321.

6   Thomas Merton, *Contemplation in a World of Action*. New York: Doubleday Image, 1973, p. 186.

7   Martin Luther King, *Strength to Love*. London: Fontana, 1969/Philadelphia: Fortress, pp. 154–55. Reprinted by

arrangement with the heirs to the Estate of Martin Luther King, Jr., c/o Joan Daves Agency as agent for the proprietor. Copyright © 1963 by Martin Luther King Jr. Copyright renewed 1991 by Coretta Scott King.

8 Jim Garrison, *The Darkness of God: Theology After Hiroshima*. London: SCM Press, 1982, p. 161. Reprinted with permission from SCM Press.

9 Belden C. Lane, 'Spirituality and Political Commitment: Notes on a Liberation Theology of Nonviolence', *America*, 14 March 1981. Reprinted with the permission of Belden C. Lane and America Press, Inc., 106 West 56th Street, New York, NY 10019, USA. Originally published in *America*, 14 March 1981 issue. Lane's article is cited by Constance Fitzgerald OCD, 'Impasse and Dark Night' in Tilden Edwards (ed.), *Living with Apocalypse: Spiritual Resources for Social Compassion*. San Francisco: Harper & Row, 1984, p. 95. © 1984 by Shalem Institute for Spiritual Formation, Inc.

10 Thomas Merton, *Faith and Violence*. Notre Dame, 1968, pp. 271, 267. Extracts from Thomas Merton, *Faith and Violence: Christian Teaching and Christian Practice*. © 1968 by the University of Notre Dame Press. Used by permission.

11 Dietrich Bonhoeffer, *Letters and Papers from Prison*. London: SCM Press/New York: Macmillan, 1971, pp. 360, 373 (SCM edn). Extracts reprinted with permission from SCM Press Ltd., and Simon & Schuster, Inc., from *Letters and Papers from Prison*, Revised, Enlarged Edition, by Dietrich Bonhoeffer. Translated from the German by Reginald Fuller et al. Copyright © 1953, 1967, 1971 by SCM Press Ltd.

12 Madonna Kolbenschlag, 'The Feminine Face of Creation: Breaking Through Myths of Power and Spirituality', *Sojourners*, May 1991, pp. 24ff. Reprinted with permission from *Sojourners*, 2401 15th Street N.W., Washington, DC 20009, USA; (202) 328-8842.

13 Rosemary Radford Ruether, 'Christian Quest for Redemptive Community', *Cross Currents*, Spring 1988, p. 9. Reprinted with permission from *Cross Currents*, College of New Rochelle, NY 10805-2308, USA.

14 David Abalos, 'Latinos and the Sacred', *Cross Currents*, Fall 1986, pp. 314, 307. The article was adapted from the (then forthcoming) book *Latinos in the United States: The Sacred and the Political*. Notre Dame: University Of Notre Dame Press, 1988. Copyright © 1986 by the University of Notre Dame Press. Used by permission.

CHAPTER 2
Thomas Merton
'The Unmasking of an Illusion'

1 Walter Conn, *Christian Conversion: a Developmental Interpretation of Autonomy and Surrender*. Mahwah: Paulist, 1986, p. 166. Extracts reprinted by permission of the copyright holder Paulist Press. Copyright © Paulist Press 1986.

2 Thomas Merton (ed. William Shannon), *The Hidden Ground of Love: Letters on Religious Experience and Social Concerns*. New York: Farrar, Straus & Giroux, 1985, p. 10. Excerpts from *The Hidden Ground of Love* by Thomas Merton, edited by William H. Shannon. Copyright © 1985 by the Merton Legacy Trust. Reprinted by permission of Farrar, Straus & Giroux, Inc.

3 From Merton's (as yet unpublished) 'St Bonaventure Journal', and cited by Michael Mott, *The Seven Mountains of Thomas Merton*. London: SPCK/Boston: Houghton Mifflin Co., 1984, p. 172. Reprinted with permission.

4 Thomas Merton, *New Seeds of Contemplation*. New York: New Directions, 1962, p. 6. In the UK the work is published as *Seeds of Contemplation*. Extracts from [New] *Seeds of Contemplation* are used with the permission of the publishers: Anthony Clarke Publishers, Wheathampstead, Hertfordshire; and New Directions Publishing Corporation, New York.

5 Merton, *New Seeds*, p. 131.

6 Merton, *New Seeds*, p. 187.

7 Merton, *New Seeds*, pp. 227–28.

8 Thomas Merton, *Thomas Merton in Alaska*. New York: New Directions, 1989, pp. 139–40. Reprinted with permission

of New Directions Publishing Corporation and Laurence Pollinger Ltd.

9 Thomas Merton, *Conjectures of a Guilty Bystander*. Garden City, New York: Doubleday Image, 1968, pp. 156-57. Reprinted with permission.

10 Merton, *Hidden Ground*, p. 501.

11 Thomas Merton, *Contemplation in a World of Action*. Garden City, New York: Doubleday Image, 1973, p. 169.

12 Thomas Merton, *The Monastic Journey*. Garden City, New York: Doubleday Image, p. 43.

13 See Thomas Merton, *Eighteen Poems*. New York: New Directions, 1985.

14 For the story of the relationship see Mott, *Seven Mountains*, pp. 435-54. See also John Howard Griffin, *Follow the Ecstasy*, Fort Worth, Texas: JHG editions/Latitudes Press, 1983; now published in a new edition by Orbis Books, Maryknoll, New York. Griffin was the original choice for Merton's official biographer but died before his work was completed. The (almost) completed section covering the years 1965-68 contains much of interest. It is Griffin who names the person Mott refers to simply as 'S' as Margie Smith.

15 Merton, *World of Action*, pp. 219ff.

16 Merton, *World of Action*, p. 208.

17 Merton, *World of Action*, pp. 225-26.

18 Merton, *World of Action*, p. 228.

19 Merton, *World of Action*, pp. 226-27.

20 Mott, *Seven Mountains*, p. 564.

21 Merton, *Hidden Ground* (13 April 1967), p. 115.

CHAPTER 3
Dietrich Bonhoeffer
'As If God Were Not Given'

1 Eberhard Bethge, *Dietrich Bonhoeffer: Man of Vision, Man of Courage*. London: Wm Collins/New York: Harper & Row, 1970, pp. 154-55. © 1970 by William Collins Sons Co. and Harper & Row Publishers Inc.

2 Dietrich Bonhoeffer, *The Cost of Discipleship*. London: SCM Press/New York: Macmillan, 1959, p. 49 (SCM edn). Reprinted with permission of SCM Press Ltd., and Simon & Schuster, Inc., from *The Cost of Discipleship* by Dietrich Bonhoeffer, translated from the German by R. H. Fuller, with some revision by Irmgard Booth. Copyright © 1959 by SCM Press Ltd.

3 Bonhoeffer, *Discipleship*, p. 272.

4 Dietrich Bonhoeffer, *Ethics*. London: SCM Press/New York: Macmillan, 1965, pp. 64–65. Reprinted with the permission of SCM Press Ltd., and Simon & Schuster, Inc., from *Ethics* by Dietrich Bonhoeffer, translated from the German by Neville Horton Smith. Copyright 1955 by SCM Press Ltd. Copyright 1955 by Macmillan Publishing Company.

5 Dietrich Bonhoeffer, *Life Together*. London: SCM Press/New York: Harper & Row, 1954, p. 67 (SCM edn). In Bonhoeffer's case, the former was true as can be seen from his subsequent life story. Extracts from *Life Together* reprinted with permission from SCM Press Ltd.

6 Bonhoeffer, *Life Together*, p. 85.

7 Bonhoeffer, *Ethics*, p. 173.

8 Bonhoeffer, *Ethics*, p. 197.

9 Bonhoeffer, *Ethics*, p. 204. As far back as 1932, Bonhoeffer could claim that 'the possibility of judging whether our action is good lies alone in Christ, the present and future one. All other "secure" possibilities, which appear to give continuity to the action, are to be rejected: 1. the orders of creation; 2. conscience; 3. a Christian principle of love; 4. the situation itself; 5. laying claim to the forgiveness of sins; 6. the Law, even in the form of the Sermon on the Mount.' 'Gibt es eine christliche Ethik?', 1932 seminar reconstructed from students' manuscripts, cited by Larry Rasmussen in William J. Peck (ed.), *New Studies in Bonhoeffer's Ethics*. New York: Edwin Mellen Press, 1987, p. 112. Used with permission.

10 Bonhoeffer, *Letters and Papers*, pp. 17, 7.

11 Robin W. Lovin, *Christian Faith and Public Choices*.

Philadelphia: Fortress Press, 1984, pp. 143-45. Reprinted from *Christian Faith and Public Choices* by Robin W. Lovin, copyright © 1984 Fortress Press. Used by permission of Augsburg Fortress.

12   The first time in the letter of 8 June 1944, although he does not yet use the term to describe it (pp. 324ff).

13   Bonhoeffer, *Letters and Papers*, p. 341.

14   Bonhoeffer, *Letters and Papers*, p. 360.

15   Bonhoeffer, *Letters and Papers*, p. 360.

16   Bonhoeffer, *Letters and Papers*, p. 168.

17   Bonhoeffer, *Letters and Papers*, p. 381.

18   Bonhoeffer, *Letters and Papers*, p. 164.

19   Bonhoeffer, *Letters and Papers*, p. 234.

20   See Bonhoeffer, *Letters and Papers*, pp. 299-300. This version is taken from Kelly and Nelson (eds.), *A Testament of Hope: The Essential Writings of Dietrich Bonhoeffer*. San Francisco: HarperCollins, 1990. © 1990 by Geffrey B. Kelly and F. Burton Nelson. Kelly and Nelson's rendering of the 'two things' as 'prayer and action by the just person on behalf of people', although clumsy, is more faithful to Bonhoeffer's intention than the translation in *Letters and Papers* which renders it 'prayer and righteous action'. The latter reading focuses on the righteousness of the individual whereas Kelly and Nelson correctly seek to emphasize the individual's service of the other.

21   Bonhoeffer, *Letters and Papers*, p. 381.

22   Bonhoeffer, *Letters and Papers*, p. 381.

23   Bonhoeffer, *Letters and Papers*, p. 382.

24   Bonhoeffer, *Letters and Papers*, p. 382.

25   Bonhoeffer, *Letters and Papers*, pp. 347-48.

CHAPTER 4
Etty Hillesum
'At One with All Existence'

1   Etty Hillesum, *Etty: A Diary 1941-43*. London: Triad-Grafton/New York: Washington Square Press, 1985, p. 10

(Grafton edn). English translation © Jonathan Cape Ltd, 1983. Extracts used with permission.

2 Hillesum, *Diary*, pp. 88, 176.
3 Hillesum, *Diary*, p. 170.
4 Hillesum, *Diary*, p. 175.
5 Hillesum, *Diary*, p. 234.
6 Hillesum, *Diary*, p. 243.
7 Hillesum, *Diary*, p. 165.
8 Hillesum, *Diary*, p. 227.
9 Hillesum, *Diary*, p. 101.
10 Hillesum, *Diary*, p. 102.
11 Robert McAffee Brown, 'Two Worlds: Beauty and Oppression', *Christian Century*, 2 April 1980, p. 380. Copyright © 1980 Christian Century Foundation. Reprinted by permission from the 2 April 1980 issue of *Christian Century*.
12 Hillesum, *Diary*, p. 152.
13 Hillesum, *Diary*, p. 229.
14 Hillesum, *Diary*, p. 173.
15 Hillesum, *Diary*, p. 182.
16 Hillesum, *Diary*, p. 173.
17 Hillesum, *Diary*, p. 197.
18 Hillesum, *Diary*, p. 225. The entry continues: 'There are so many empty houses, and I shall prepare them all for You, the most honoured lodger. Please forgive this poor metaphor.'
19 Hillesum, *Diary*, p. 207.
20 Hillesum, *Diary*, p. 189.
21 Hillesum, *Diary*, p. 190.
22 See Hillesum, *Diary*, p. 118.
23 Hillesum, *Diary*, p. 161.
24 Hillesum, *Diary*, p. 52.
25 Hillesum, *Diary*, p. 125.
26 Hillesum, *Diary*, p. 131.
27 See Hillesum, *Diary*, p. 100.
28 Hillesum, *Diary*, p. 236.
29 Hillesum, *Diary*, p. 232.
30 For similar thoughts on the vulnerability of God, compare

Hillesum, *Diary*, pp. 192 and 197 with Dietrich Bonhoeffer, *Letters and Papers*, pp. 348–49.

31 Etty Hillesum, *Letters from Westerbork*. London: Grafton, 1988, p. 23. Reprinted with permission of Pantheon Books Inc.

CHAPTER 5
A New Way of Seeing
Contemplation and Connectedness

1 Peter C. King, 'A Baptist Looks at Thomas Merton' (a lecture given to the Downside Colloquom, April 1992), *Downside Review*, July 1992, pp. 195–208.

2 See William Rees Mogg, *The Times*, 15 February 1993.

3 Thomas Merton, *The Seven Storey Mountain*. London: SPCK/San Diego: Harcourt Brace, 1990. Excerpt from *The Seven Storey Mountain* by Thomas Merton, copyright © 1948 by Harcourt Brace and Company and renewed 1976 by the Trustees of the Merton Legacy Trust. Reprinted by permission of the publishers.

4 James Fowler's theory of faith stages has been applied to Merton by Walter Conn, *Christian Conversion*. The individuative stage marks the transition from a faith at 'second hand', adhering to conventional concepts and formulations (conventional) to a faith which is understood and expressed in terms of one's own words and experiences.

5 See William Shannon, 'Thomas the Person', address to The Merton Conference, London: 2 May 1987.

6 I am indebted to American Lutheran Minister John Schramm for this insight, especially in his tape 'The Contemplative Vision'. Holden Village, Chelan, WA 98816, USA.

7 Merton, *New Seeds*, pp. 131, 129.

8 Merton, *New Seeds*, p. 51.

9 John Garvey, 'Asceticism and the Evil One: Why Do We Refuse to Acknowledge Evil?', *Commonweal*, 22 May 1987, pp. 311–12. Reprinted with permission.

10   See some of the essays in Merton, *Faith and Violence*. One particular essay in the collection, *Seeds of Destruction*, brought a robust response from church historian Martin Marty which criticized Merton for making such a rash prophecy from the enclosed environment of the monastery. How could *he* know where America was heading? Yet four years later, Marty found himself overtaken by events, and offered a public apology to Merton, admitting that Merton did indeed have a clearer understanding of American society than he did himself.

11   Christopher Nugent, 'The Ecumenical Orthodoxy of St John of the Cross', *New Oxford Review*, December 1991, pp. 13–18. Reprinted with permission. It is this article which is the source for the Flannery O'Connor epigraph with which this work begins.

12   Bonhoeffer, *Ethics*, p. 200.

13   Bonhoeffer, *Ethics*, p. 197.

14   See Bonhoeffer, *Letters and Papers*, p. 300.

15   The Confessing Church was an alternative church structure to the 'German Christians'. They represented those Christians from the state Church who refused to submit themselves theologically and organizationally to the Nazi regime. The June 1936 issue of *Evangelische Theologie* carried a paper by Bonhoeffer in which he stated that 'Whoever knowingly separates himself from the Confessing Church in Germany separates himself from salvation'. Cited by Bethge, *Dietrich Bonhoeffer*, p. 430. Not surprisingly, Bonhoeffer's words incited much controversy.

16   Bonhoeffer, *Ethics*, pp. 90, 95.

17   Bonhoeffer, *Ethics*, p. 210.

18   Bonhoeffer, *Letters and Papers*, p. 7.

19   Dietrich Bonhoeffer, *Fiction from Prison*. Philadelphia: Fortress Press 1981, p. 77. Reprinted from *Fiction from Prison* by Dietrich Bonhoeffer, copyright © 1981 Fortress Press. Used by permission of Augsburg Fortress.

20   Bonhoeffer, 'After Ten Years', *Letters and Papers*, p. 17.

21   Bonhoeffer, *Letters and Papers*, p. 360.

22   Constance Fitzgerald, 'Impasse and Dark Night', p. 103.

23 The phrase is from Larry Rasmussen, 'New Dynamics in Theology', *Christianity and Crisis*, 16 May 1988, p. 178.

24 Hillesum, *Diary*, p. 246.

25 Hillesum, *Diary*, p. 231.

26 Thomas Merton (ed. Robert E. Daggy), *The Road to Joy: Letters to New and Old Friends*. New York: Farrar, Straus & Giroux, 1989, p. 348. Excerpts from *The Road to Joy* by Thomas Merton (ed. Robert E. Daggy). Copyright © 1989 by the Merton Legacy Trust. Reprinted by permission of Farrar, Straus & Giroux, Inc.

27 James A. Carpenter, *Nature and Grace: Toward an Integral Perspective*. New York: Crossroad, 1988, p. 84. Copyright © 1988 by James A. Carpenter. Reprinted by permission of The Crossroad Publishing Co., New York.

28 Merton, *Asian Journal*. New York: New Directions, 1973, pp. 317, 315. The quote comes from a paper entitled 'Monastic Experience and East-West Dialogue', prepared for an address in Calcutta, October 1968. Reprinted with permission of New Directions Publishing Corporation and Laurence Pollinger Ltd.

29 Bonhoeffer, *Letters and Papers*, p. 380 (notes dated July/August 1944).

30 Matthew 25:31–46.

31 Conn, *Christian Conversion*, p. 64.

32 Conn, *Christian Conversion*, p. 64.

33 Spretnak, *States of Grace*, p. 24.

34 Spretnak, *States of Grace*, p. 27.

CHAPTER 6
A New Way of Doing Theology
The 'New Paradigm'

1 Walter Capps, *The Monastic Impulse*. New York: Crossroad, 1983, p. 46.

2 Douglas John Hall, *Thinking the Faith: Doing Theology in a North American Context*. Minneapolis: Augsburg, 1989, p. 362. Reprinted from *Thinking The Faith* by Douglas John Hall, copyright © 1989 Augsburg Fortress.

3 Thomas Kuhn, *Postscriptum*, 1969, p. 175. Cited by Hans Kung, 'What Does a Change of Paradigm Mean?', in Kung and Tracy (eds.), *Paradigm Change in Theology A Symposium for the Future*. Edinburgh: T.&T. Clark, 1989, p. 215, translated by Margaret Köhl. Authorized English translation of *Theologie – Wohin?* and *Das Neue Paradigma von Theologie* © T.&T. Clark Ltd, 1989. Original German Edition © Benziger Verlag Zürich-Köln and Gütersloher Verlagshaus Gerd Mohn, Gütersloh. By permission of T.&T. Clark and New York: Crossroad Publishing Co., 1989.

4 Kung and Tracy, *Paradigm Change*, p. 4.

5 Kung and Tracy, *Paradigm Change*, p. 311.

6 See Kung and Tracy, *Paradigm Change*, pp. 205ff (Jerald Brauer).

7 See Kung and Tracy, *Paradigm Change*, pp. 220ff (Jurgen Moltmann).

8 See Kung and Tracy, *Paradigm Change*, pp. 367ff (Langdon Gilkey).

9 Edward Schillebeeckz in Kung and Tracy, *Paradigm Change*, p. 318.

10 Johann Baptist Metz in Kung and Tracy, *Paradigm Change*, p. 366 (footnote 30).

11 Larry Rasmussen, 'New Dynamics in Theology', *Christianity and Crisis*, 16 May 1988, p. 178. Extracts used by permission of the author.

12 Rasmussen, 'New Dynamics', p. 178.

13 Rasmussen, 'New Dynamics', p. 179.

14 Rasmussen, 'New Dynamics', p. 179.

15 Rasmussen, 'New Dynamics', p. 179.

16 Rasmussen, 'New Dynamics', p. 183.

17 Teresa of Avila, cited and discussed by Merton in the essay, 'The Humanity of Christ in Monastic Prayer', collected in *The Monastic Journey*. New York: Doubleday Image, 1978, pp. 121ff.

18 Rebecca S. Chopp, *The Praxis of Suffering: An Interpretation of Liberation and Political Theologies*. Maryknoll: Orbis, 1986, p. 19. Reproduced with permission.

19 Chopp, *Praxis*, p. 25.

20 Chopp, *Praxis*, p. 27.
21 Chopp, *Praxis*, p. 63.
22 Chopp, *Praxis*, p. 62.
23 See the collection of articles on the address in *Christianity and Crisis*, 15 July 1991, pp. 220ff.
24 *Christianity and Crisis*, p. 222.
25 *Christianity and Crisis*, p. 222.
26 *Christianity and Crisis*, pp. 222–23.
27 *Christianity and Crisis*, p. 223.
28 See also such works as the dialogues between 'New Age' physicist Fritjof Capra and Benedictine monk David Steindl-Rast, *Belonging to the Universe: Explorations on the Frontiers of Science and Spirituality*. San Francisco: HarperCollins, 1991. Or, very differently, theologian James McLendon's work on biography as theology, most recently, *Systematic Theology: Ethics*. Nashville: Abingdon, 1986.
29 See for example Mark Kline Taylor, *Remembering Esperanza: A Cultural–Political Theology for North American Praxis*. Maryknoll: Orbis, 1990, pp. 1ff.